Contents

Farming in Britain

Settlements

Going Places

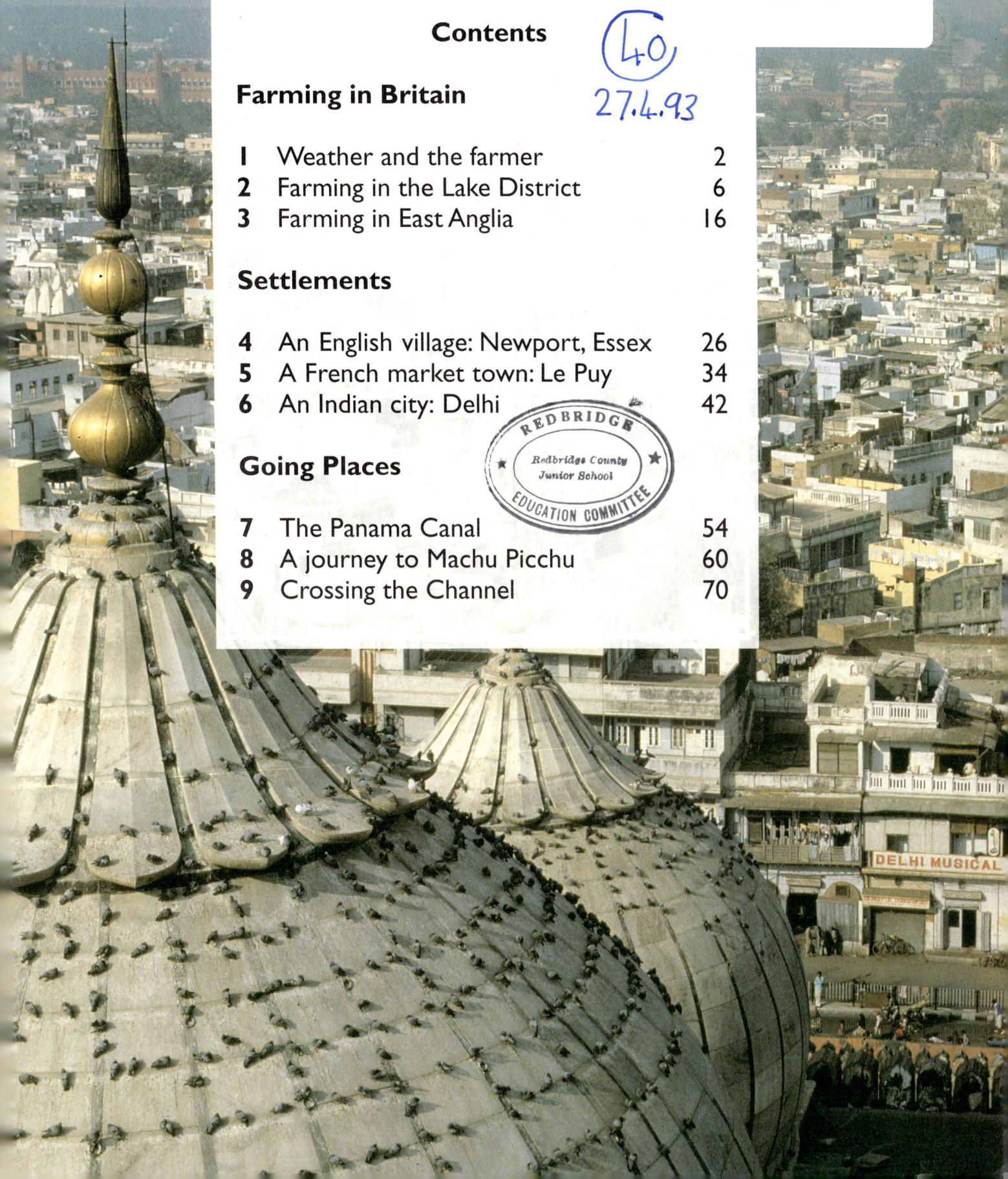

Weather and the farmer

What's the weather like?

Every day on TV we are told what sort of weather we will get for the next 24 hours (A). This is called a weather forecast.

Look at map B. It shows a weather forecast for England and Wales on 4 March. The symbols on the map tell us what the weather will be like in different areas.

C tells us what the weather forecaster said about the weather shown on map B.

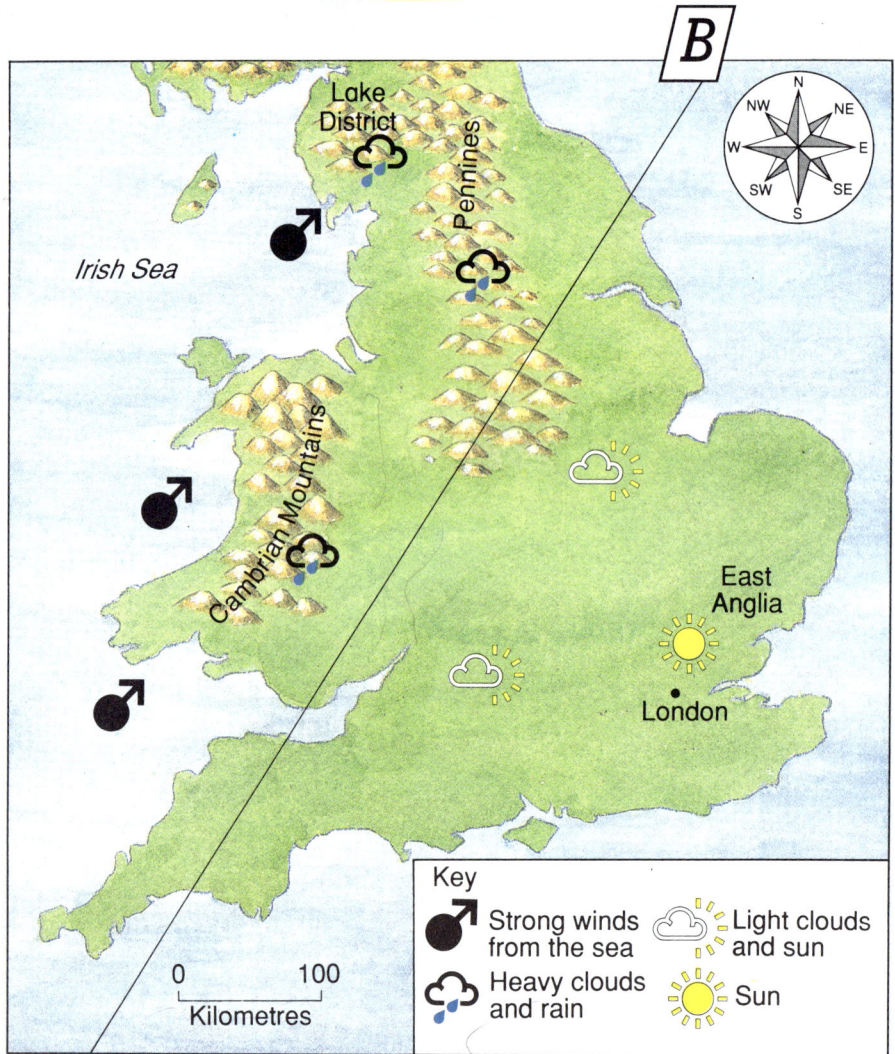

"There will be a lot of rain tomorrow and for the rest of the week.
Rain will be heavy in the mountains of the north and the west. It will be cool and windy.

On the lowlands of the south and the east, there may be a few showers, but it will be mostly dry.
In East Anglia and the London area it will be warm and sunny."

Key

Strong winds from the sea

Heavy clouds and rain

Light clouds and sun

Sun

Look at B and C.

1a Name three areas that will have rain on 4 March.

1b Which side of the country will have more sunshine?

1c From which direction are the winds blowing across Wales and England?

1d Where will it be warm and sunny?

1e In which part of England are there more lowland areas?

1f If you lived in the Lake District, what sort of weather would you have on 4 March?

The winds that blow across Britain usually come from the west. They often bring rain clouds to the western side of the country.

There are mountainous areas in many parts of western Britain. When the rain clouds rise above these mountains, they get cooler, and rain falls (B).

D

D shows part of the Lake District in north-west England. When the west winds blow across the Lake District mountains, a lot of rain falls.

East Anglia is a lowland area in eastern England (E). Here, the weather is much drier and warmer than in the Lake District.

E

Look at B, D and E.

2a Name a part of Britain that has the same sort of weather as the Lake District.

2b Why do places in the north and west of Britain get more rain than places in the south and east?

2c The line on map B divides the country into two parts. In what ways are the two parts different?

2d Write about the differences you can see in D and E.

Weather and farming

Plants and crops need sun and rain to make them grow. This is why the weather is very important to farmers.

If the weather is too cold, too wet or too dry, crops may not grow. Wind and snow may also harm crops and animals.

A, B and C tell us what three different farmers say about the sort of weather they do not like.

A sheep farmer in the Lake District
"I don't like heavy snow in winter. It means I have to carry food for the sheep up to the hills and sometimes the sheep are buried in the snow. Digging out the sheep can be very hard work."

A fruit farmer in south-east England
"We have a good crop of apples this year. Last year we had frost at the end of Spring. It killed the blossom on the trees, so we had very little fruit. The other thing we hate is stormy weather in summer. The winds can blow the fruit off the trees before it is ripe."

A grain farmer in East Anglia
"I don't like strong winds at harvest time. Storms can flatten the crops and make it difficult to cut them."

Weather forecasts are very important for farmers. *D* tells us what a grain farmer says about them.

D

E

"At harvest time, we always listen carefully to the weather forecast. If it says the weather will be dry for a few days, we hire the combine harvesters. We cut the grain all day and all night until the job is done. (*E* and *F*)

Last year, the forecasters were wrong. The forecast was for dry weather but we had heavy rain. We wasted money hiring the combines. The ground was too wet for them, and the wind and rain flattened the wheat.

Most years are fine, and the forecasters get it right." (*F*)

F

Heavy rain can damage crops, and it can also be harmful to animals. If the rain falls heavily for several days, rivers may overflow their banks and flood the farmland (*G*).

Cows and sheep cannot eat the grass in flooded fields, and they may drown in deep flood water.

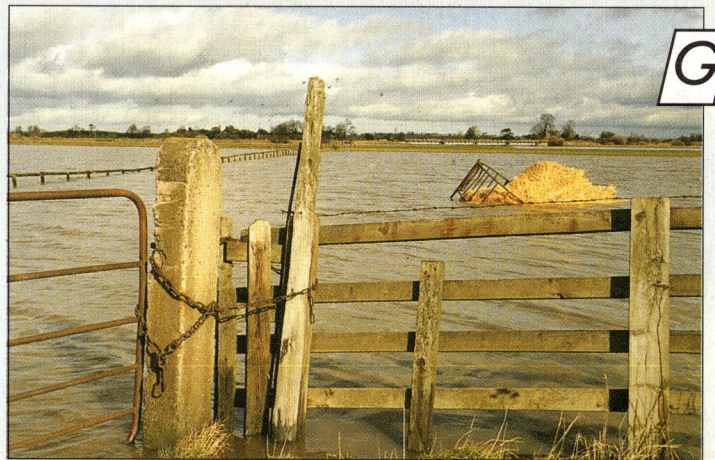
G

Look at *A*, *B*, C and *D*.

1   Which farmers do not like strong winds? Why not?

Look at *D* and *E*.

2   What might happen to a combine harvester on very wet ground?

Look at *G*.

3   How could a weather forecast help the farmer to save his cows from the floods?

4   Choose one of the photographs and write about what it shows.

Farming in the Lake District

A farm in Great Langdale

Chris Benson is a farmer in the
Lake District. He farms sheep and cattle.
He runs Harry Place Farm, which is in the
Great Langdale valley (*B* and *C*).

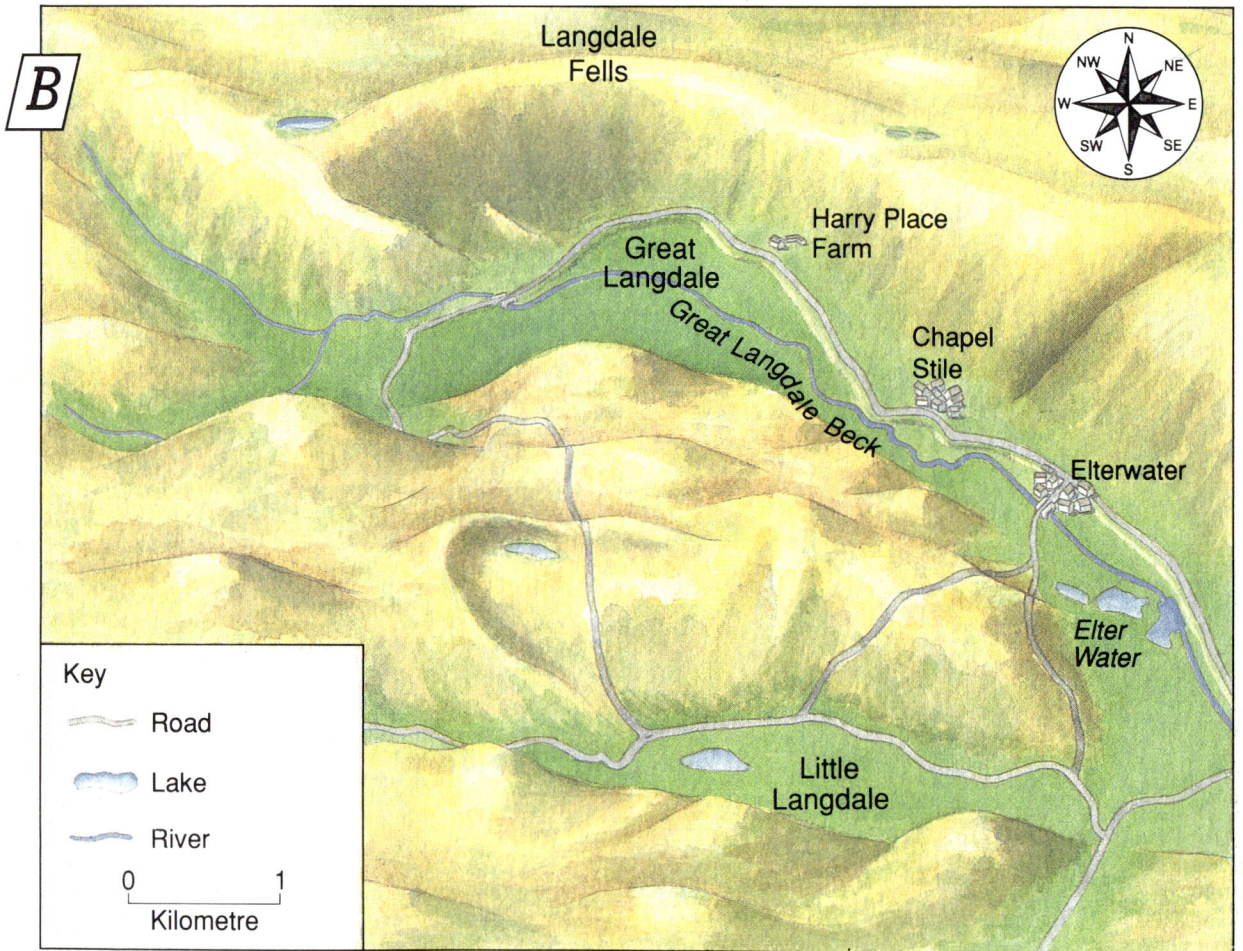

Key

Road

Lake

River

0   1
Kilometre

Langdale Fells

Harry Place Farm

Great Langdale

Great Langdale Beck

Chapel Stile

Elterwater

Elter Water

Little Langdale

Many farms in the Lake District are sheep and cattle farms. There are no grain farms in the mountains (D).

D

"It is too wet to grow crops like wheat in Great Langdale. There are more days with rain than without rain (F).
The west winds bring rain to the mountains (E).
We have more rainfall than any other part of England.
The steep slopes and poor soils also make it difficult to grow grain. We could not drive a combine harvester up the steep slopes."

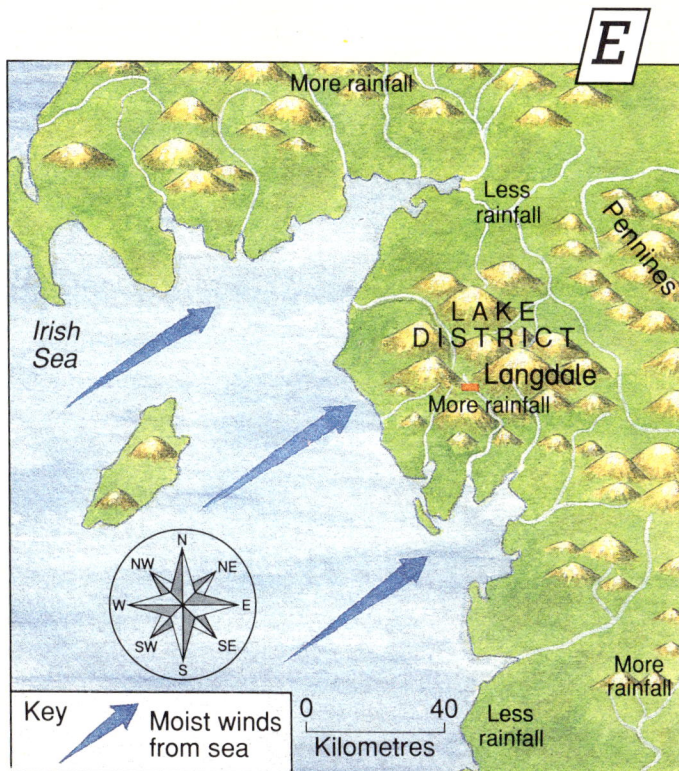

E

More rainfall

Less rainfall

Pennines

Irish Sea

LAKE DISTRICT

Langdale

More rainfall

More rainfall

Less rainfall

Key — Moist winds from sea

0 — 40 Kilometres

The weather in Great Langdale

Months	J	F	M	A	M	J	J	A	S	O	N	D
Temperature	Cool		Mild			Warm				Mild		Cool
Number of days with rain	22	18	19	15	16	13	17	19	19	20	21	22

F

Wet all year round, especially in winter

Look at B.

1 Imagine you live at Harry Place Farm. Write directions to tell a friend how to get from Lake Elter Water to the farm. Use the compass and the scale on map B to help you.

Look at F.

2a Which month has the least rainfall?

2b In which months are there more days with rain than without rain?

2c In which seasons of the year is the weather mild?

Look at D, E and F.

3a Give two reasons why Chris Benson does not grow grain crops.

3b Why does Great Langdale have such a high rainfall?

G

"We have one good crop - it is grass. Grass grows well in cool, wet weather.

In the spring, when the grass is long (H), we cut it and pack it into plastic bags (I). By the winter, the grass inside the bags has turned into silage. We give this to the sheep and cows to eat.

After the grass has been cut (J), we put the lambs and their mothers (ewes) into the fields. The other sheep stay high up on the fells, unless the winter weather is very bad. Then we bring them down near to the farm."

H

I

J

Look at H, I and J.	Look at K and L.
4a What is grass used for on Harry Place Farm?	5a Name the three sorts of land on the farm.
4b Why does grass grow so well in Great Langdale?	5b Which part of the farmland has the most fields? Why?
4c When do the sheep and cattle eat the silage?	5c Why are the dairy cows kept in the fields near the farm and not on the fells?
4d Why are the lambs kept in fields close to the farm?	

Like most farms in the Lake District, Harry Place Farm is made up of different sorts of land (*K* and *L*).

The flat land near the farm on the valley floor is called **inbye** land. This is the best land. The dairy cows, ewes and lambs are kept in the grass fields on inbye land for part of the year.

Above the farm, the slopes are steeper and the soils are thinner and less rich than in the valley. This part of the farmland is called **intake** land.

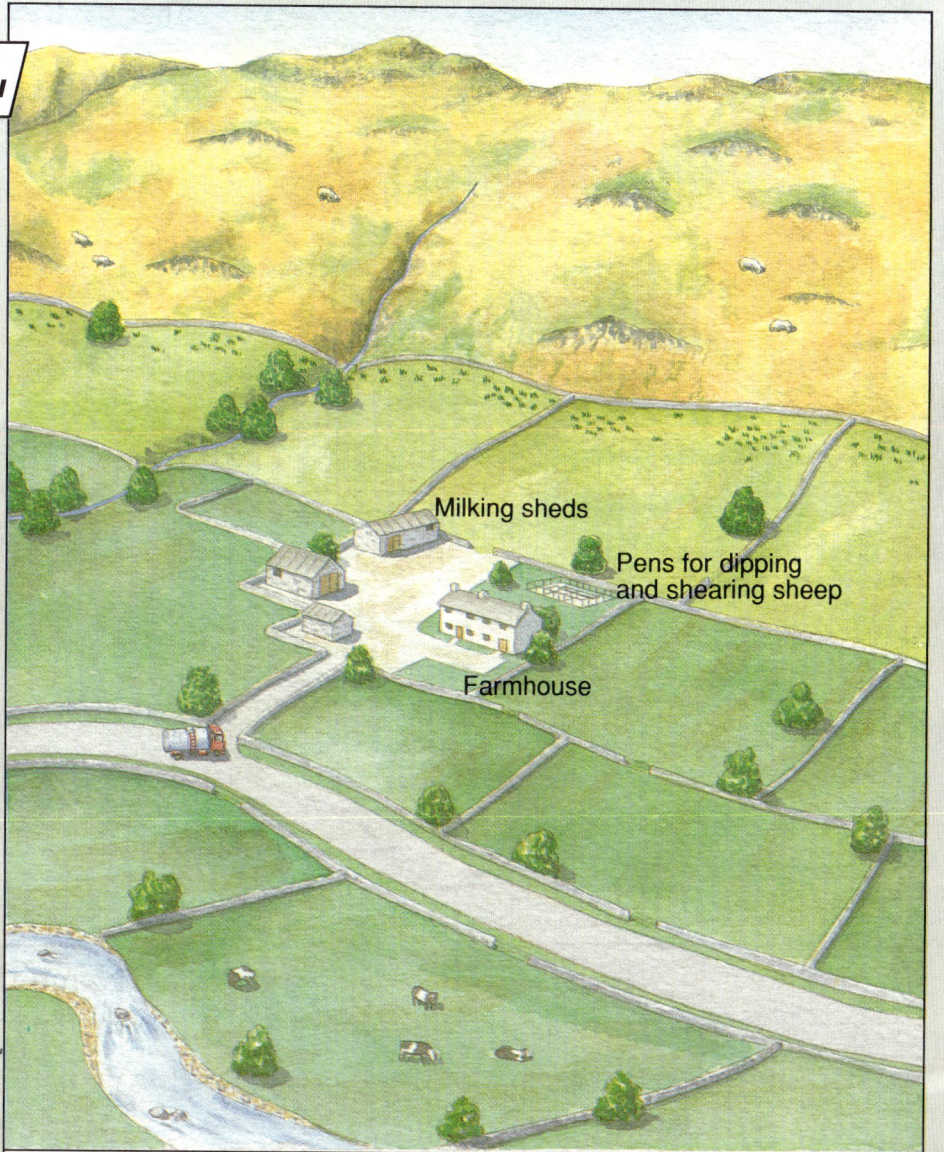

Milking sheds

Pens for dipping and shearing sheep

Farmhouse

Above the intake land are the slopes of the **fells**. There is enough grass for the sheep to eat, but it is too steep and rocky for the cows to climb up here.

Key

Fell land	Stone walls	
Intake land	Bracken	 River
Inbye land	Stream	

A year on Harry Place Farm

A tells you what happens to the sheep and cows during the year on the farm.

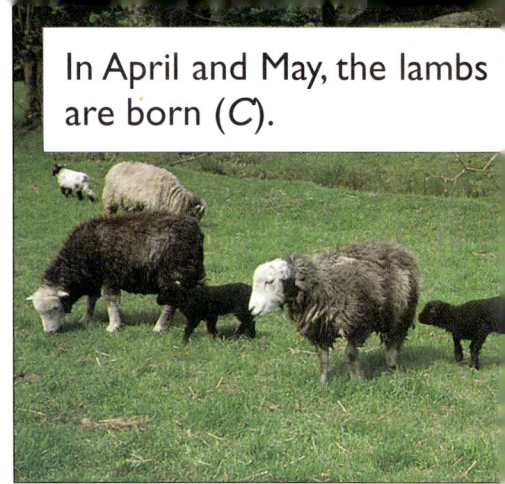

In April and May, the lambs are born (*C*).

Winter is often a busy time. If the snow is deep, food has to be taken to the sheep up on the fells (*B*).

In summer, the cows graze on the good grass in the inbye fields. Every day, they are taken from the fields to the milking shed on the farm (*F*).

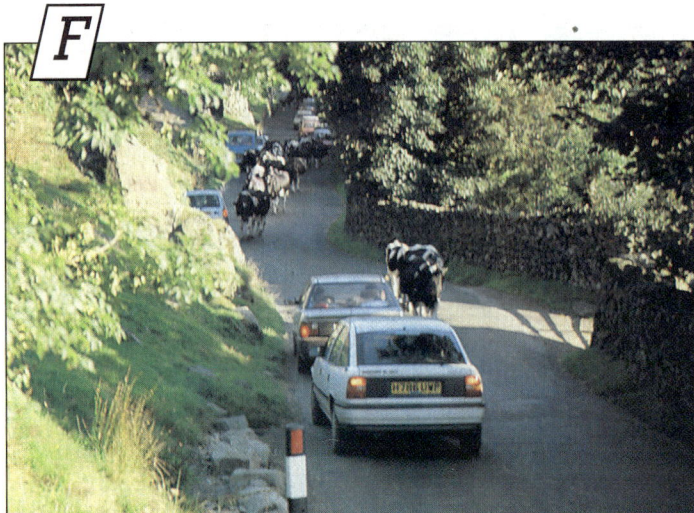

B

A

Sheep

| All sheep on fells Weaker ewes brought down to valley | Lambing time | Ewes with lambs in valley | Shea and dippi |

| Jan | Feb | Mar | Apr | May | Ju |

Cattle

| Cattle indoors fed on hay and silage | Hay and silag collected |

F

G

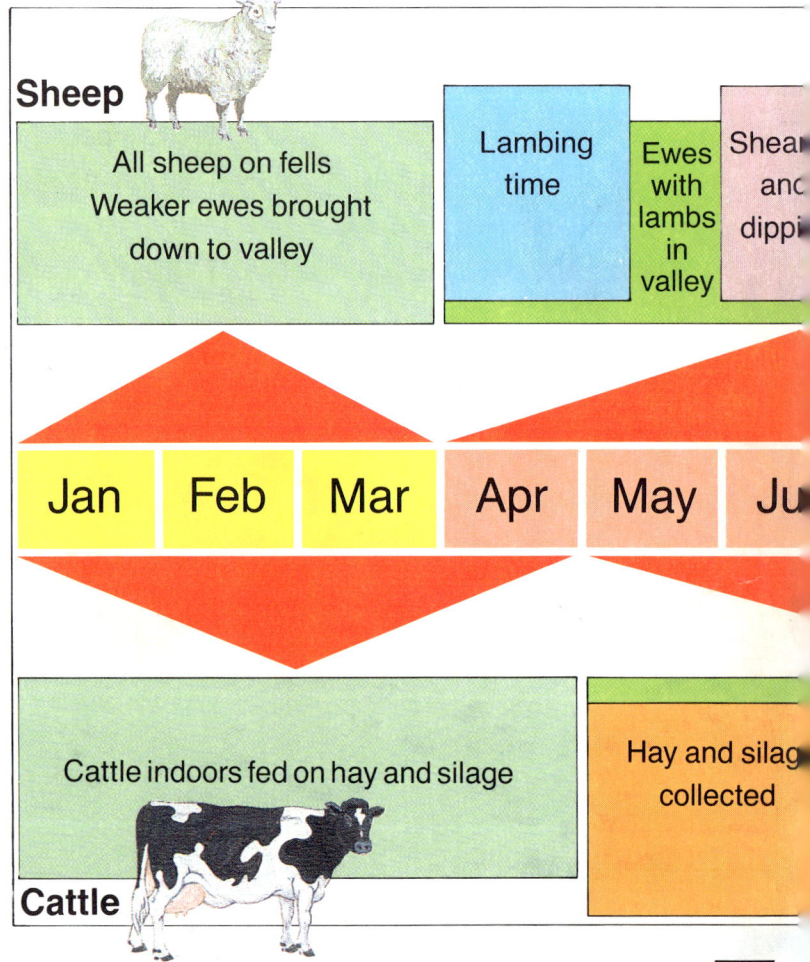

Chris Benson's son Tom often helps with the cows (*G*).

June is the month when the sheep are sheared and dipped (D). They are also marked (E). The farmers use different marks so that they know which sheep on the fells belong to them.

C

E

Lamb sales

Ewes with twin lambs in valley; the rest on fells

All sheep on fells

Ewes tupped (mated with rams)

| Jul | Aug | Sep | Oct | Nov | Dec |

Cattle grazed near farm: brought in for milking

Cattle indoors

1a For how many months are the cattle kept indoors?

1b In which months are the lambs sold?

1c List the jobs that are done on the farm in April, June and November.

1d Choose a job you would like to do on the farm. Write about the job, and say why you would like to do it.

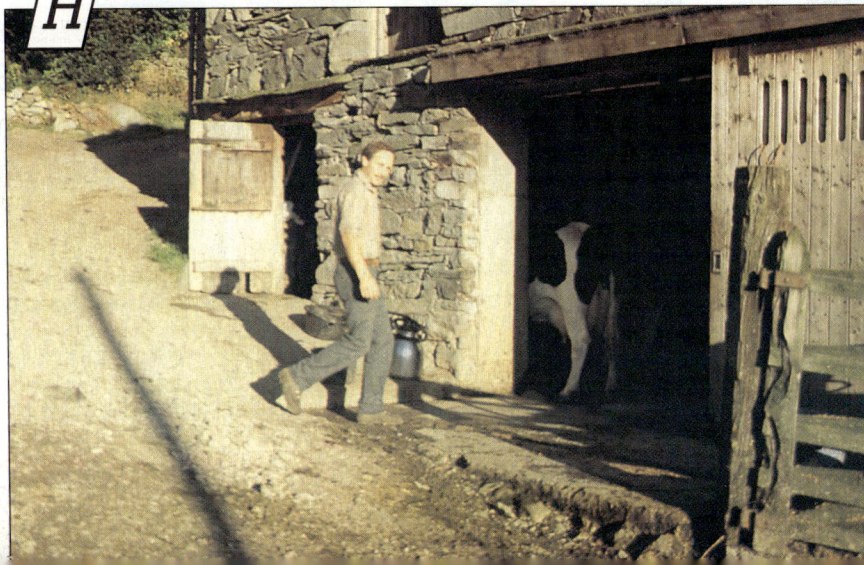

H

In H you can see Chris Benson going into the shed to milk the cows.

In winter, the cows are kept inside. They feed on hay and on silage.

Earning a living on a farm

The money Chris Benson makes comes from selling his sheep, sheep's wool and cows' milk (A). He makes nearly half of his money from the sheep.

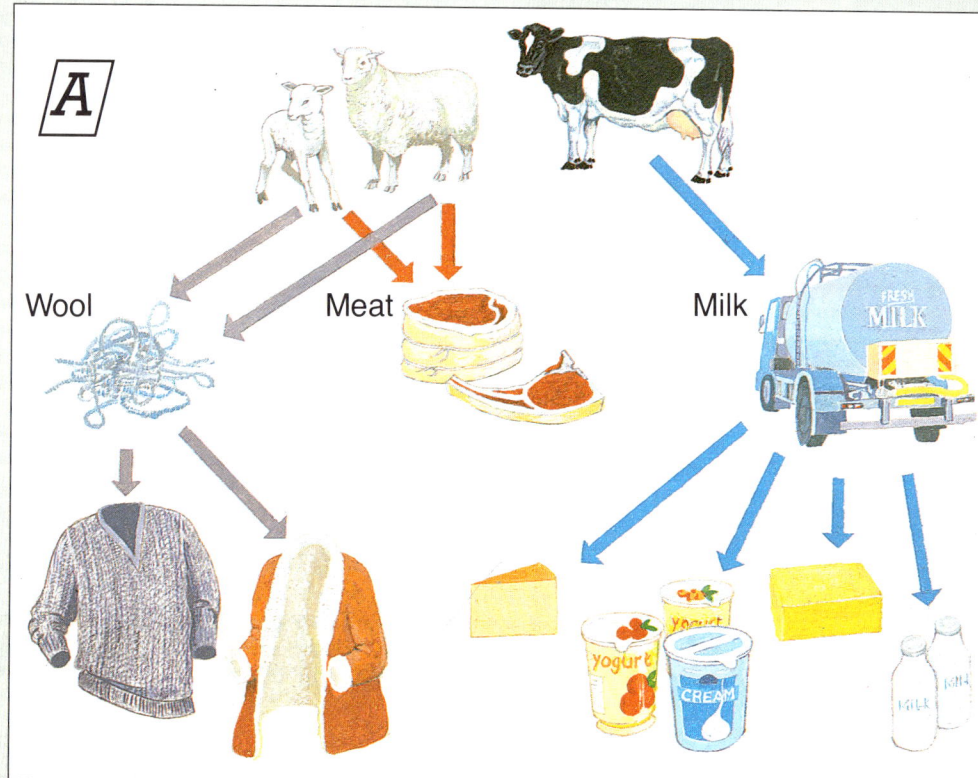

Most of the lambs are sold at sales called auctions (B).

The cows are milked every day, and the milk is collected from the farm by a milk tanker. The tanker is almost as wide as the road from the farm (C).

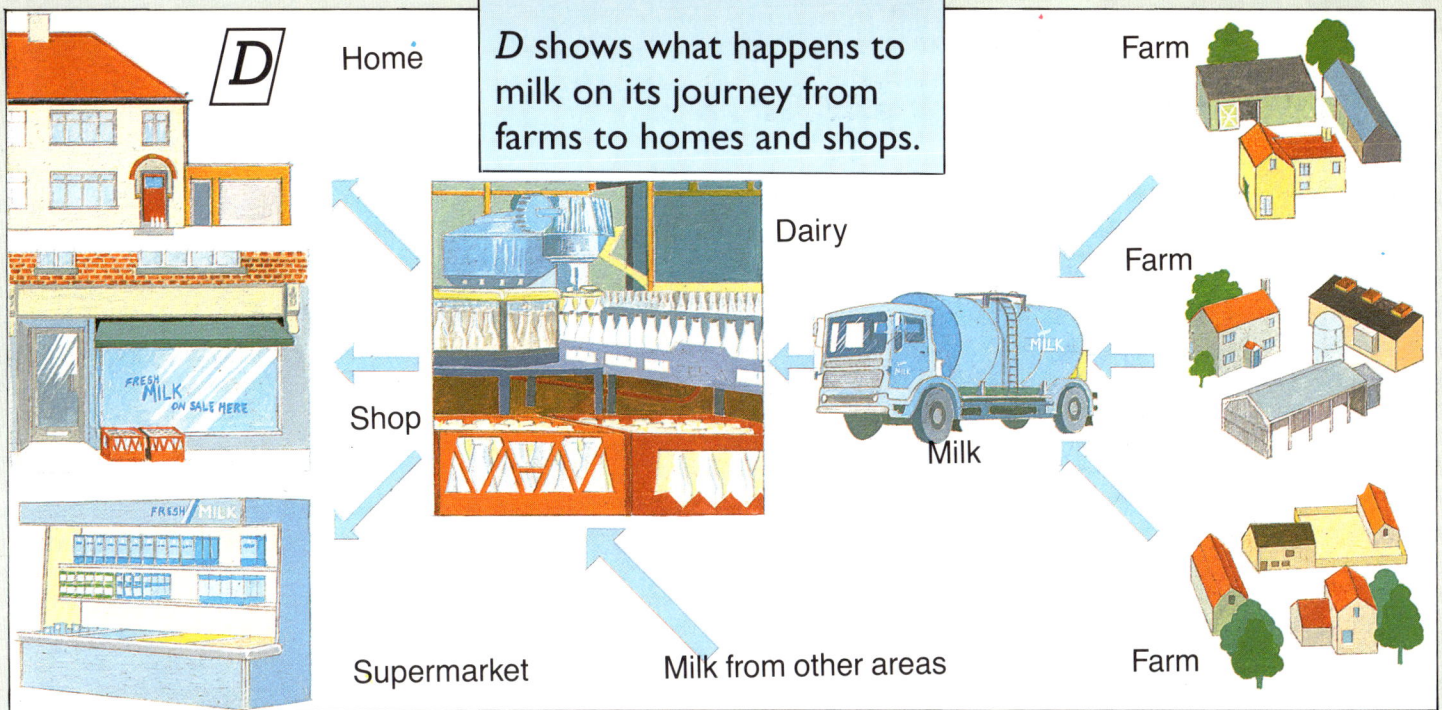

D shows what happens to milk on its journey from farms to homes and shops.

Home

Farm

Dairy

Farm

Milk

Shop

Supermarket

Milk from other areas

Farm

Farms cost a lot of money to run. The farmhouse and farm buildings cost money to run and to repair. The farmer's family needs money to live on, and there are wages to pay to farm workers.

On Harry Place Farm there are two tractors (*E*). These were expensive to buy, and they need fuel as well as repairs and new parts.

E

Look at *A* and *B*.

1a   List three things that Chris Benson sells to make money.

1b   List the products shown in A that come from sheep and cows.

Look at *C* and *D*.

2a   What problems could be caused by the milk tanker?

2b   What do you think happens inside a dairy?

2c   Write about what *D* shows.

3a   List three things that Chris Benson has to buy for the farm.

3b   Add three more things to your list of expenses for Harry Place Farm.

Tourists in the Lake District

A

Every year, thousands of tourists visit the Lake District. They come to look at the beautiful scenery, and to walk on the fells. Sometimes, walkers damage the farmland (*A*).

B

The National Trust owns a lot of land in the Lake District (*B*). One of its jobs is to repair worn footpaths (*A*).

C

Visitors may harm animals. The sheep in *C* may be run over. Other sheep may be chased or killed by visitors' dogs (*D*).

D

LAMBING SEASON!

Do not disturb the sheep

Keep dogs under close control
(ON A LEAD, PLEASE!)

THANK YOU

E

Tourists may spoil the countryside, but they can also help local people to earn a living.

Local people work in shops, hotels, pubs (*E*) and cafés (*F*) in the area.

F

STICKLEBARN
Bar & Eating House Tel LANGDALE 356
Traditional Real Ales & Good Company
BAR SNACKS
Try our Eating House for Breakfasts, Snacks, Grills AND ALL YOUR HOT AND COLD MEALS REQUIREMENTS
COFFEE · TEA · SOFT DRINKS · ICES
PACKED LUNCHES AVAILABLE — ALL PARTIES CATERED FOR

Some local farmers also earn money from visitors who come to stay on the farm.
Farm holidays are very popular in the Lake District (*G*).

Look at *A*, *C* and *D*.

1a List three ways in which tourists may bring harm to local farmers.

1b What must visitors do to keep the sheep safe from harm?

Look at *E*, *F* and *G*.

2a Why do some farmers have visitors to stay?

2b List four sorts of people who earn money from visitors to the Lake District.

3 Would you like a holiday in the Lake District? What sort of place would you stay in, and how would you spend your time?

G

MILL BECK FARM ACCOMMODATION

15

Castle Farm

Rebecca Haylock enjoys playing with her friend Julia and the family donkey (*A*). There is plenty of space to play in. This is because Rebecca lives on a farm. The farm is in East Anglia (*B*).

Rebecca's parents (*C*) own three farms. The one where they live is named after Camps Castle. It is called Castle Farm. The castle has gone now, and so has the old village around it. The village church is still there, and so is the moat and the mound where the castle used to be. You can see these things on the plan of Castle Farm (*D*).

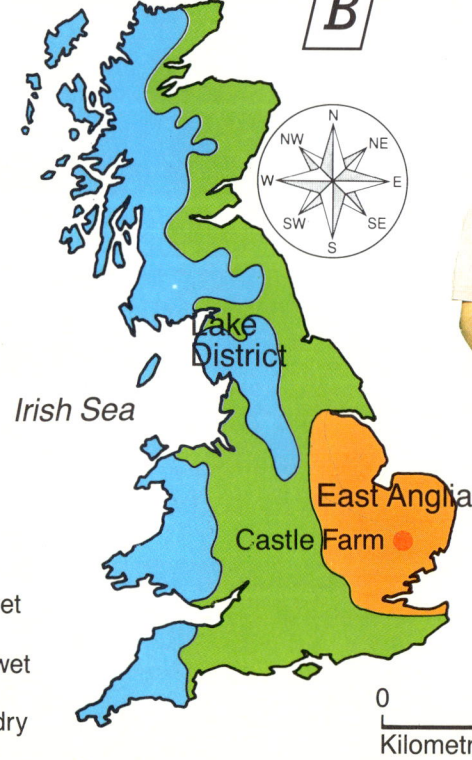

Rainfall in Britain

Lake District

Irish Sea

East Anglia

Castle Farm

Key

Very wet

Fairly wet

Fairly dry

0   100
Kilometres

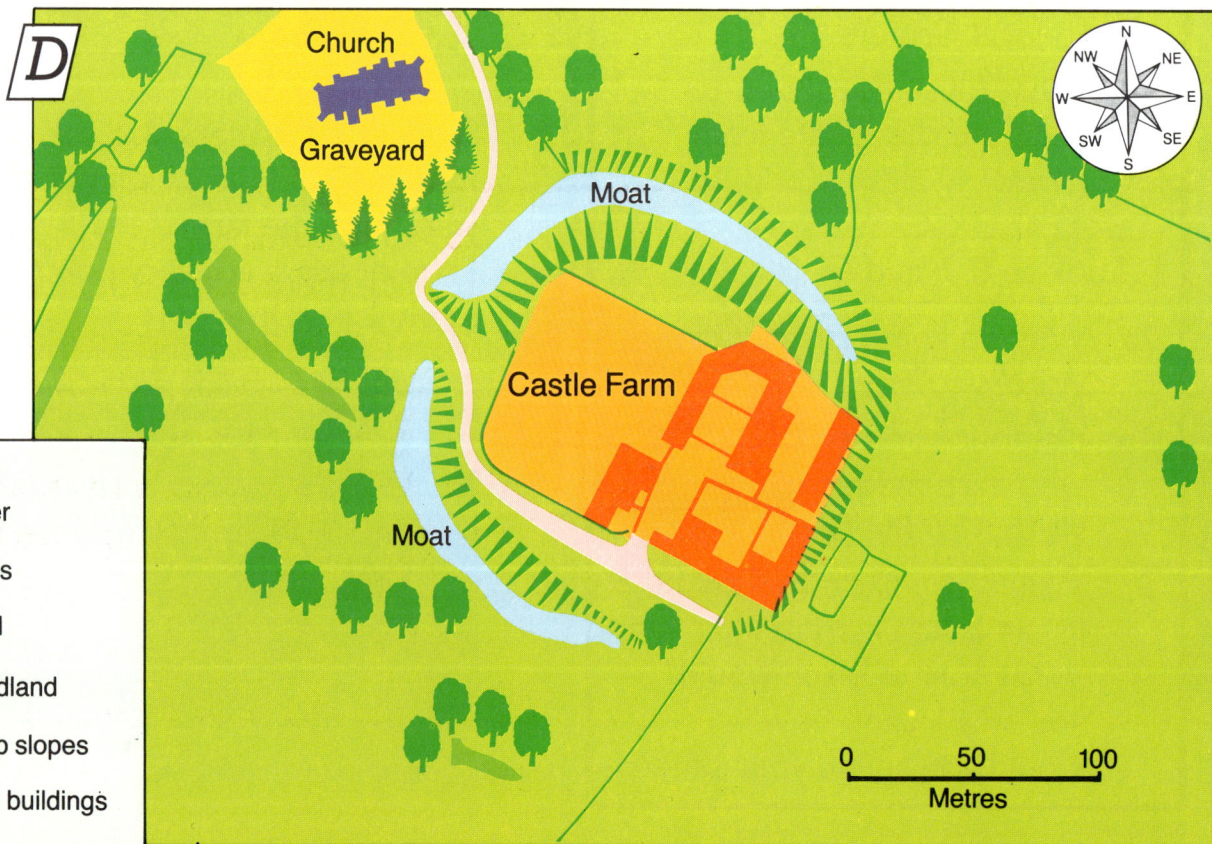

Church

Graveyard

Moat

Moat

Castle Farm

Key

Water

Fields

Road

Woodland

Steep slopes

Farm buildings

0   50   100
Metres

16

The nearest village to the farm is also named after the castle. It is called Castle Camps and is one kilometre away from the farm. You can see the village, the farm and the old church in E.

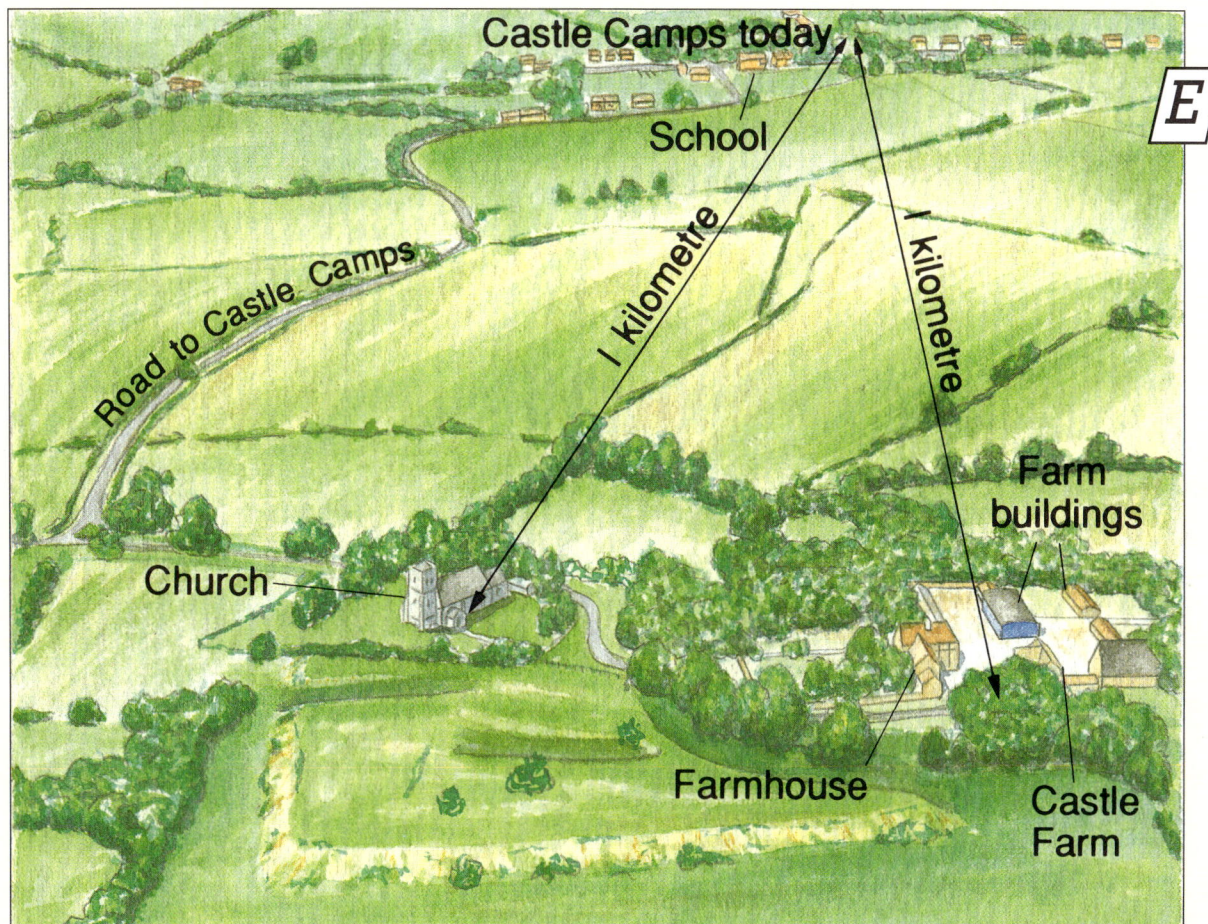

Castle Camps today
School
E
Road to Castle Camps
1 kilometre
1 kilometre
Farm buildings
Church
Farmhouse
Castle Farm

Look at B.

1 Is East Anglia an area of
a) high or low rainfall?
b) highland or lowland?

Look at D and E.

2a What can you find on D and E that tell you that a castle once stood where Castle Farm is now?

2b One building from the old village is still there. What is it?

2c Look at the shapes of the moat and the farm buildings in plan D. What are the shapes like?

2d What would you see around you on a walk from the village to the old church?

Different types of farming

You can see the Haylocks' three farms on map **A**.

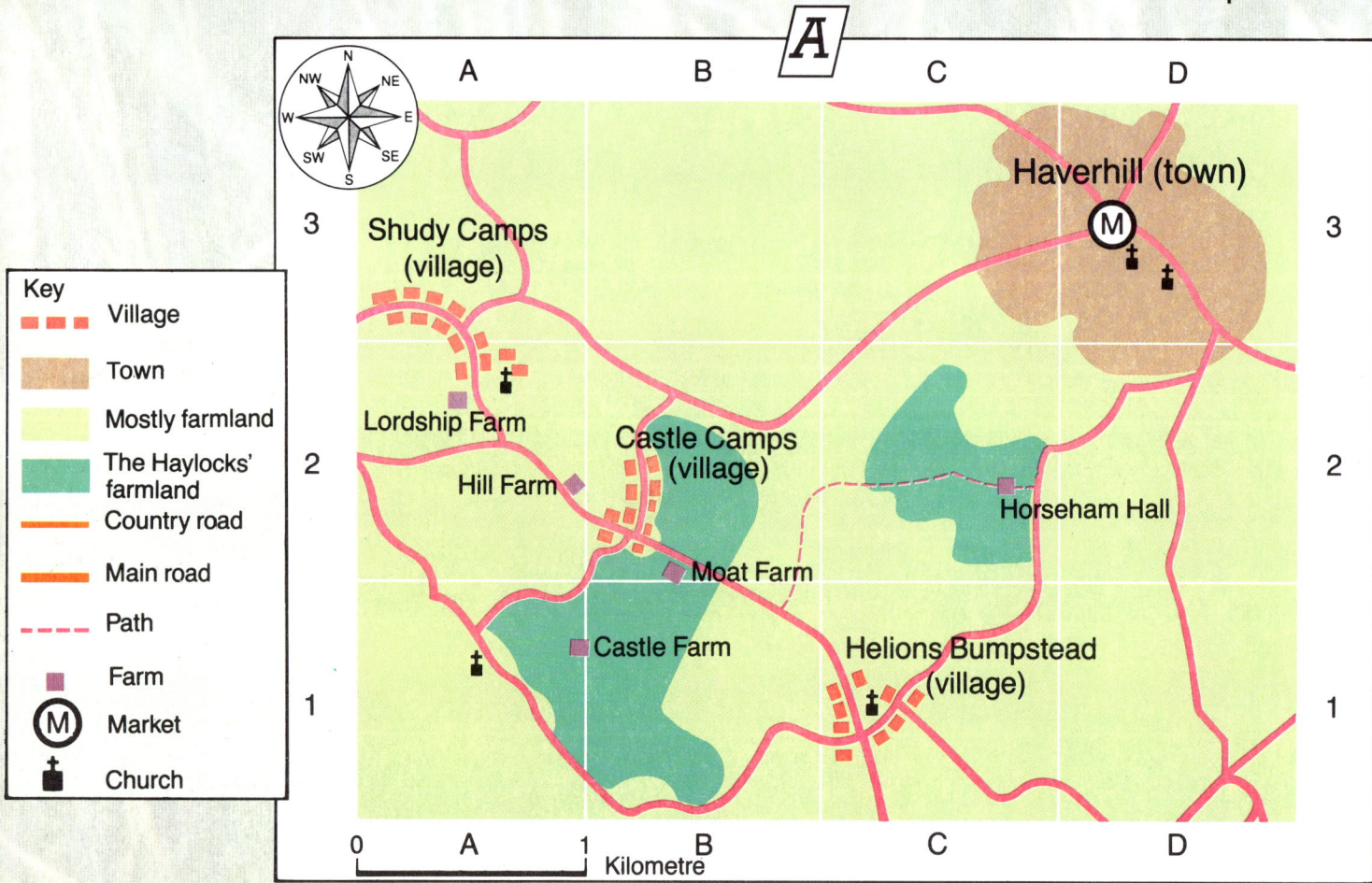

A

Key
- 🟥 Village
- 🟫 Town
- 🟩 Mostly farmland
- 🟩 The Haylocks' farmland
- Country road
- Main road
- Path
- 🟪 Farm
- Ⓜ Market
- ⛪ Church

Shudy Camps (village)

Lordship Farm

Hill Farm

Castle Camps (village)

Moat Farm

Castle Farm

Haverhill (town)

Horseham Hall

Helions Bumpstead (village)

0   A   1   B   C   D
Kilometre

Types of farming

B

Growing crops	Growing crops and keeping animals	Keeping animals
Arable farming	Mixed farming	Pastoral farming

The three farms are used for different things. Some of the land is used for growing crops. This is called **arable** farming (B).

Farms which keep animals and grow crops are called **mixed** farms (B).

Many of the fields are used for grazing animals. This is called **pastoral** farming (B). C shows some dairy cows grazing on grass, or pasture, at Castle Farm.

C

18

Three different types of crop are grown on the Haylocks' farms. These are grain crops, root crops and green vegetables.

Barley   Wheat   Oats

Wheat (D), barley (E) and oats (F) are all grain crops. They change colour from green to yellow as they ripen.

Sugar beet (G) is the only root crop grown on the Haylocks' farms. Some other farms nearby also grow potatoes.

Peas are grown on Horseham Hall farm (A), and the Haylocks also grow beans.

Look at A.

1a Name the three farms owned by Martin and Patricia Haylock.

1b The farm in square B2 belongs to the Haylocks. What is it called?

1c In which place would you find a church and a market?

Look at B.

2a On what sort of farm would you find cows, grain crops and vegetables?

2b Draw your own picture to show what arable farming means.

Look at D, E, F and G.

3a Name two sorts of root crop.

3b Draw some green vegetables that you know. Label each one to show what it is.

A year on a mixed farm

A shows the jobs that are done in each season of the year on the Haylocks' farms. These jobs are to do with growing crops.

In East Anglia, the weather and the soils are good for growing crops (B). There is some rain in each month, and the weather is warmer and sunnier than in the Lake District (see page 2).

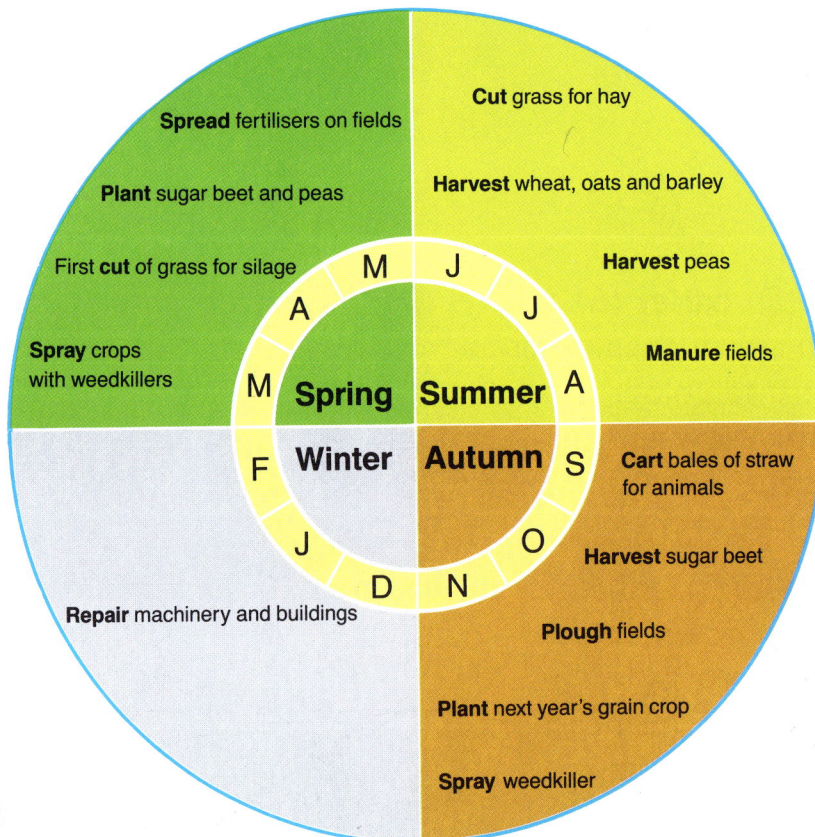

A

Spring
- **Spread** fertilisers on fields
- **Plant** sugar beet and peas
- First **cut** of grass for silage
- **Spray** crops with weedkillers

Summer
- **Cut** grass for hay
- **Harvest** wheat, oats and barley
- **Harvest** peas
- **Manure** fields

Autumn
- **Cart** bales of straw for animals
- **Harvest** sugar beet
- **Plough** fields
- **Plant** next year's grain crop
- **Spray** weedkiller

Winter
- **Repair** machinery and buildings

Months: A M J J A S O N D J F M

B

The weather at Castle Camps

Months	J	F	M	A	M	J	J	A	S	O	N	D
Temperature	Cool	Cool	Mild	Mild	Warm	Warm	Very warm	Very warm	Warm	Mild	Mild	Cool
Number of days with rain	18	14	16	12	12	10	12	12	12	15	15	20

Winter | Spring | Summer | Autumn | Winter

Key
- Wet months
- Drier months

Patricia Haylock tells us about the weather at Castle Camps (C).

C

"In most years, the weather is good and the grain ripens on time. Sometimes we get too much rain in August. This causes problems at harvest time. If the grain gets too wet, we cannot cut it. Our soils are made of clay, and they get wet and sticky after heavy rain. This makes it difficult to drive the combine harvesters on to the fields."

The grain is cut when it is ripe at the end of the summer. If the weather is too wet or too cold, the grain takes longer to ripen.

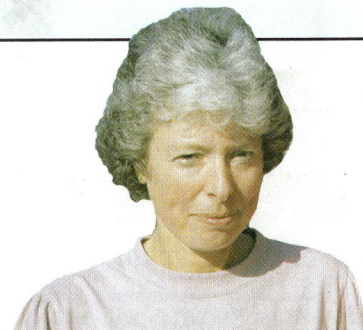

Harvest time is very busy on the farms. The combine harvesters have strong headlights so that they can work all night and day to cut the grain (D). The land is flat so the big machines can move easily around the fields.

The combine harvesters separate the stalks (straw) from the ears of the grain. The ears are blown into a waiting hopper which is pulled by a tractor (E). The straw is made into bales and used as feed and bedding for the animals (F).

Look at A.

1a In which season are the peas and the sugar beet planted?

1b In which season is the grain harvested?

1c Why is winter a good time to repair the buildings and the machines on the farms?

Look at B and C.

2a In which season is the weather warmest?

2b Which months have more days with rain than without rain?

2c Why is a wet August bad for the grain harvest?

Look at D, E and F.

3 What happens to the grain stalks after they are cut?

4 Give two reasons why East Anglia is a good place to grow grain crops.

The cows on the Haylocks'
farms are all dairy cows.
The milk they produce is
sold to a dairy.

In the summer, the cows graze
in grass fields near the farm (*G*).
Every day, they are taken from
the fields, along the farm track
(*H*) to the milking parlour (*I*).

In winter, there is not enough
grass for the cows to eat.
They are kept inside big sheds
where they eat straw, silage
and hay (*J*).

Hay is dried grass. The grass is cut in June when the weather is warm and the grass is dry. It is made into bales and stored in a barn (*K*).

Silage is made from grass too, but it is cut in April and May when the grass is still long and green.

The Haylocks own a silo (*L*) which is used to make the silage. The grass is loaded into the silo and an acid (like vinegar) is added to it. This turns the grass into rich food for the cows and pigs.

Look at *G* to *L*.

5a In which season is there the most work to do with the cows?

5b What are the differences between hay, straw and silage?

5c What might happen to the hay if the weather is very wet in June?

23

Earning a living

Robert lives on Moat Farm.
This is what he says about it (A).

A tells us something about the cost of running a farm. So does diagram B.

A "I live with my family in a rented house on Moat Farm. It is owned by Mr and Mrs Haylock. My dad works there. There are 12 men on the farm. We have 1100 pigs and 114 cows. My dad and his mate feed them every day. There is a workshop for repairing machinery. The farm has bought two new tractors and we have a new sprayer which cost £25 000."

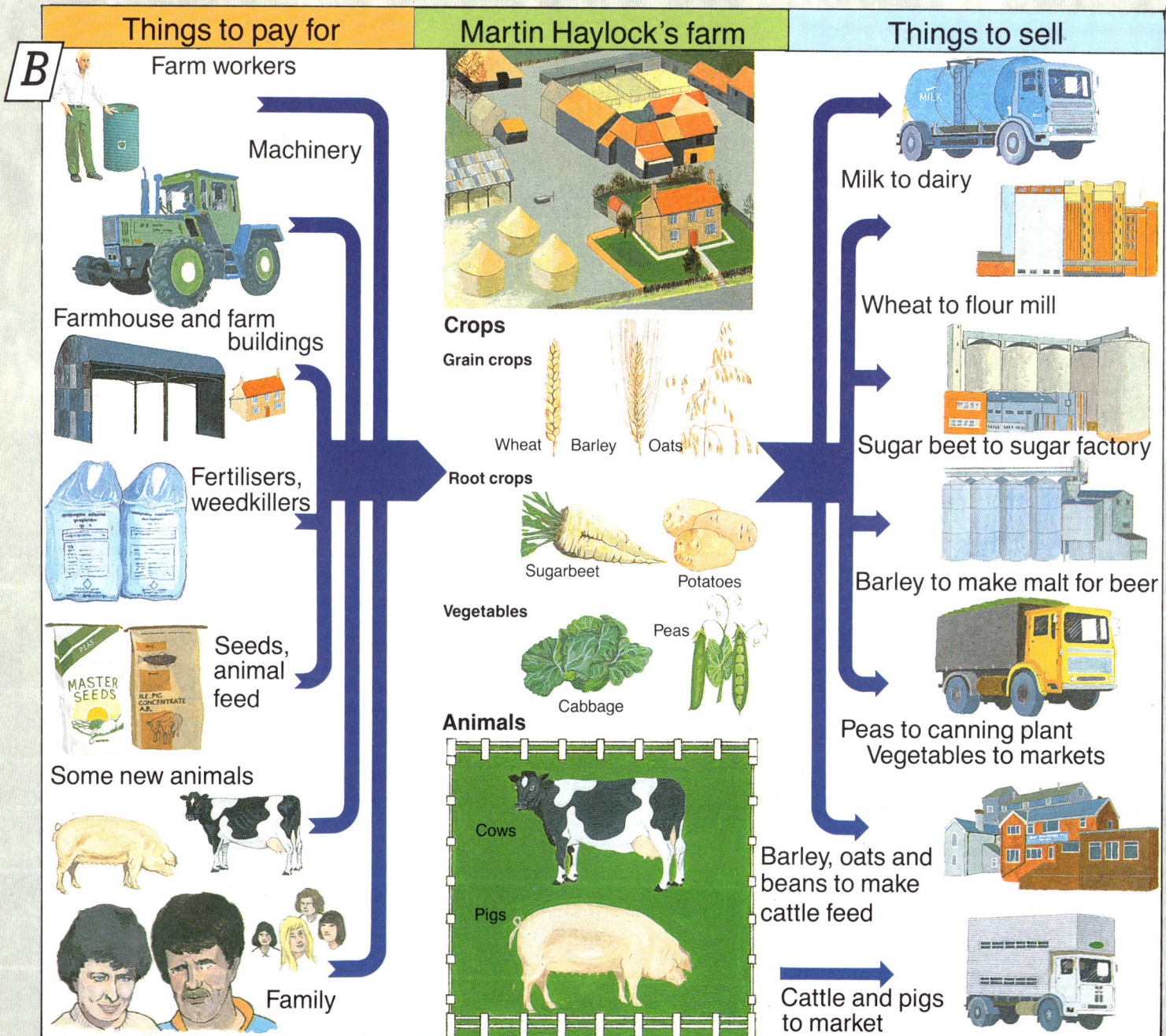

B

Things to pay for	Martin Haylock's farm	Things to sell

Things to pay for:
- Farm workers
- Machinery
- Farmhouse and farm buildings
- Fertilisers, weedkillers
- Seeds, animal feed
- Some new animals
- Family

Martin Haylock's farm:

Crops

Grain crops: Wheat, Barley, Oats

Root crops: Sugarbeet, Potatoes

Vegetables: Cabbage, Peas

Animals: Cows, Pigs

Things to sell:
- Milk to dairy
- Wheat to flour mill
- Sugar beet to sugar factory
- Barley to make malt for beer
- Peas to canning plant
- Vegetables to markets
- Barley, oats and beans to make cattle feed
- Cattle and pigs to market

The Haylocks' farms sell crops, milk and animals. This is how money is made to pay for the costs of running the three farms.

B shows the things that are sold on the Haylocks' farms. Some other farms nearby sell different things.

C

Hill Farm sells some of its
produce at a shop
on the farm (C).

D

Lordship Farm makes some
of its money by running a
riding school on its land (D).
You can see both these farms
on map A on page 18.

Look at B.

1a   Make a table like this one,
with headings in each column.

Earning	Spending

Make a list of the things the Haylocks
spend money on, and the things they
earn money from.

1b   List four products that are made
from the crops that are grown on
the Haylocks' three farms

Look at C.

2a   Make a list of the products you can
see on sale at Hill Farm shop.

2b   What things does Hill Farm
produce that the Haylocks'
farms do not?

3   Imagine that you work on
one of the Haylocks' farms.
Write a diary for a week on
the farm in winter or summer.

What is Newport like?

There are at least 16 places in Great Britain called Newport (*A*). One of these places is a village in Essex (*A* and *B*).

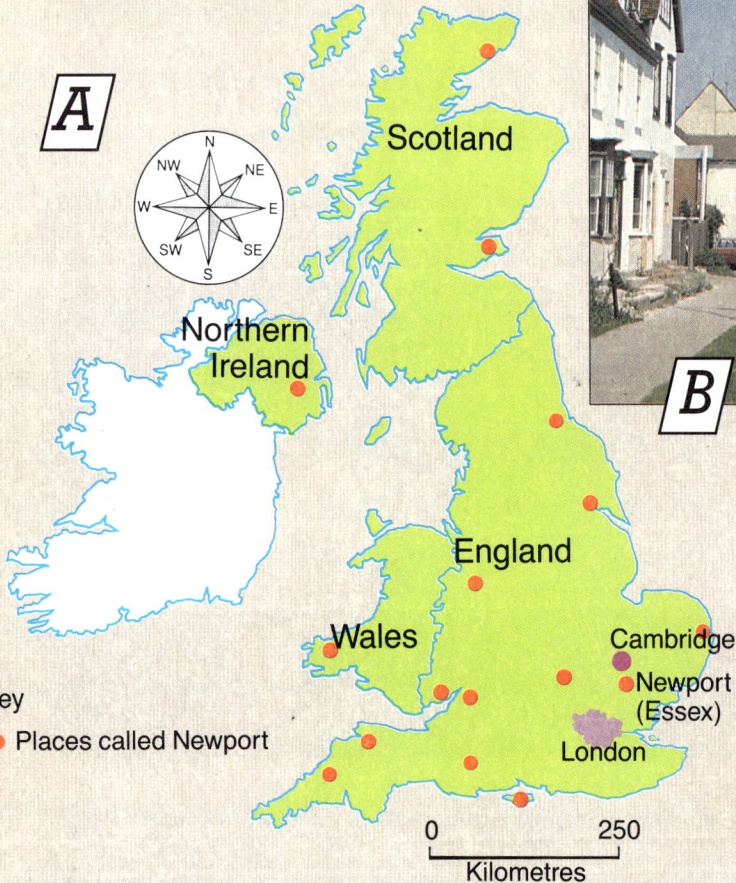

Newport, Essex, is a very old village. Monks Barn (*C*) and Saint Mary's Church (*D*) were built about 500 years ago.
The thatched cottages in *E* are also very old.

Railway

Parsonage Farm

High Street

Saint Mary's Church

F

G

Key

Buildings (mostly houses)

Farm buildings

Fields and gardens

The centre of Newport, Essex, 60 years ago

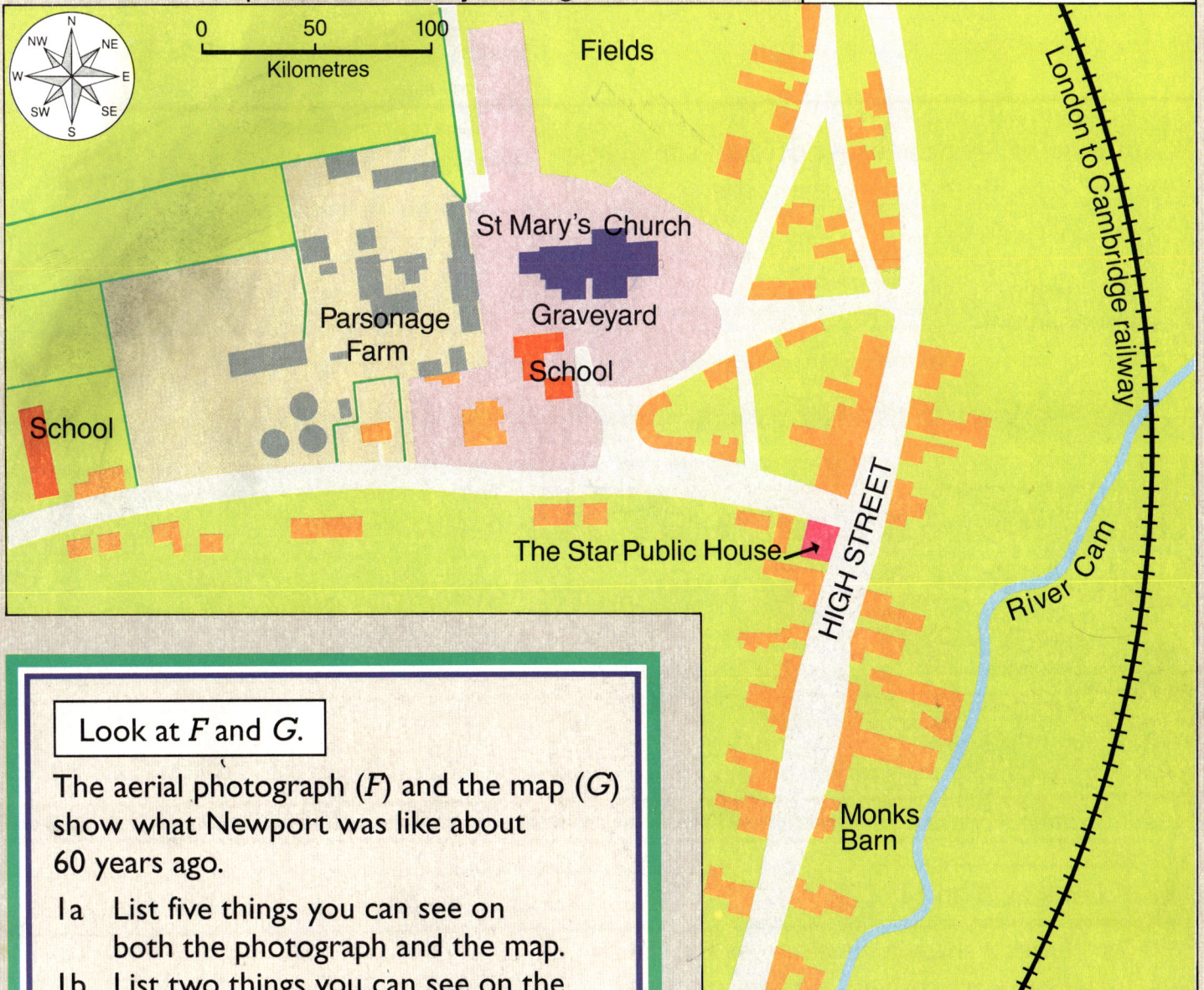

0   50   100
Kilometres

N
NW   NE
W   E
SW   SE
S

Fields

St Mary's Church

Parsonage Farm

Graveyard

School

School

The Star Public House

HIGH STREET

London to Cambridge railway

River Cam

Monks Barn

Look at F and G.

The aerial photograph (F) and the map (G) show what Newport was like about 60 years ago.

1a   List five things you can see on both the photograph and the map.

1b   List two things you can see on the map, but not on the photograph.

Newport is in the valley of the River Cam. A railway line and a road also run along the valley. You can see them on map *H*.

The railway line links London with Cambridge. Some of the trains stop at Newport.

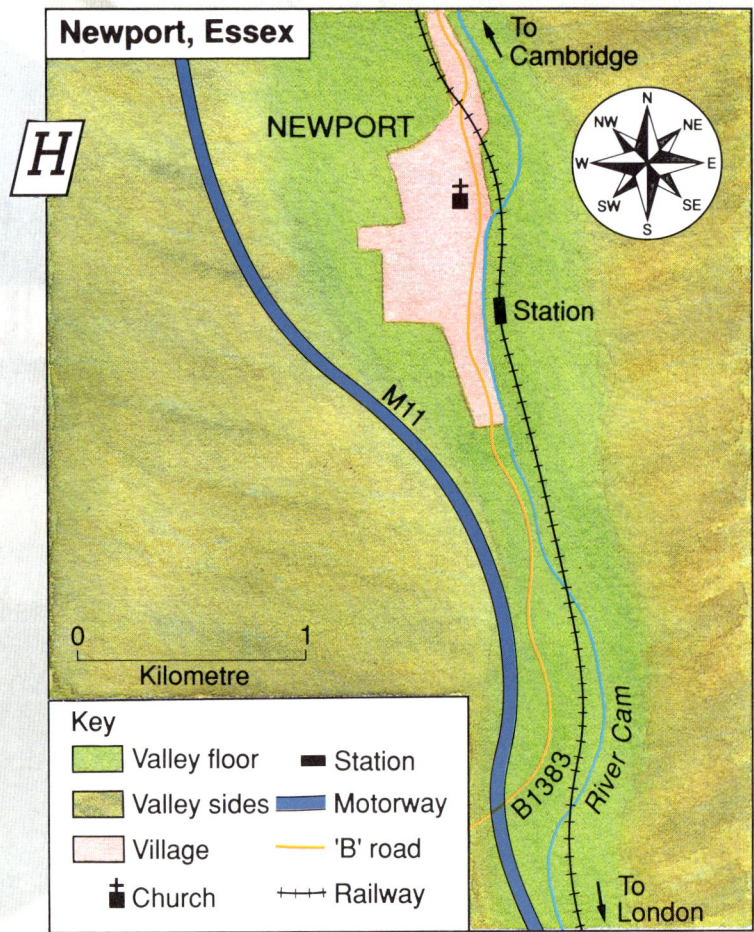

Newport, Essex

H

NEWPORT

To Cambridge

Station

M11

B1383

River Cam

To London

Key

Valley floor	Station
Valley sides	Motorway
Village	'B' road
Church	Railway

0   1
Kilometre

The drawing (*I*) is a view across the Cam river valley near Newport. You can see the M11 motorway in the distance.

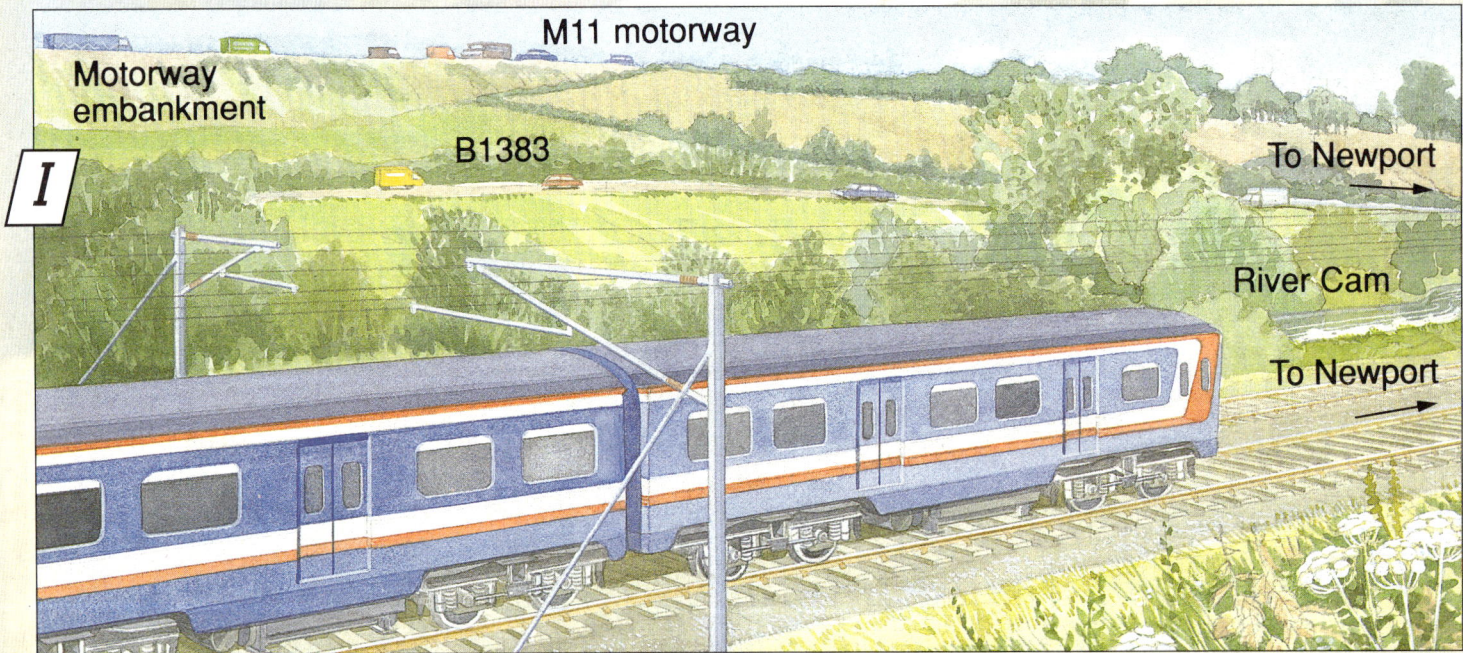

I

M11 motorway

Motorway embankment

B1383

To Newport

River Cam

To Newport

Look at *H* and *I*.

2a   Does *I* show a view across the valley from east to west, or west to east? How can you tell?

2b   Name two differences between the routes taken by the M11 and the B1383.

How has Newport changed?

When the M11 motorway was opened, it made a big difference to the people who live in Newport (*A*).

Before the motorway was built, most of the traffic between London and Cambridge used the main road through Newport. The big lorries and cars brought noise, dirt and danger to Newport High Street.

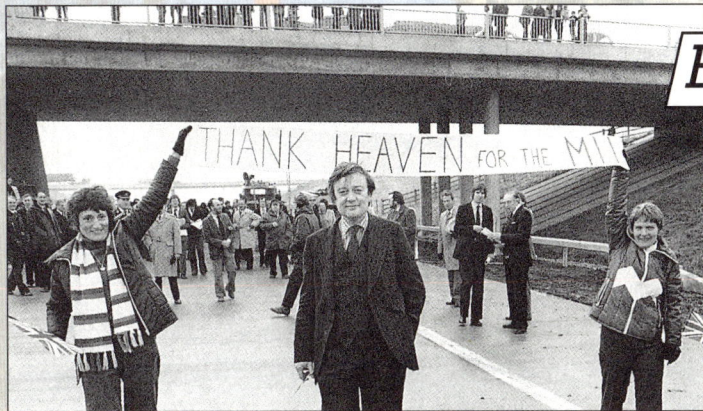

The local residents were pleased when the M11 was opened (*B*). Newport High Street is quiet now that the traffic uses the motorway.

The M11 is a very busy road. Graph *C* shows how many vehicles went on the M11 past Newport between 10.00 and 10.30 one Tuesday morning.

Vehicles on the M11 near Newport

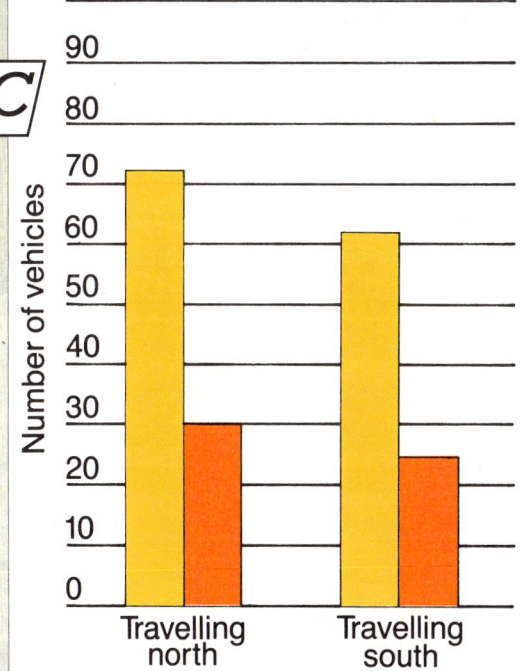

Key
Cars
Vans, lorries, coaches

Look at *C*.

1a How many vehicles travelled in each direction?

1b Did more cars travel north or south? How many more?

2 Imagine you live in a house on Newport High Street. Write about how the street changed when the M11 was built.

The motorway has changed Newport, and there have been other changes as well.

The old village shop is still there, but the house above it is now offices (D).

Part of the old house in E is used as an antique shop.

New houses have been built in the village. The ones in F are where Parsonage Farm used to be. You can see the farm in F and G on page 27.

Newport has two garages in the High Street. You can see one of them in G. Some local people do not like the garages. They think they spoil the look of the street.

> **Look at D, E, F and G.**
>
> 3a List four changes that have been made to Newport.
>
> 3b List some of the places in Newport where people work.
>
> **Look at E and F.**
>
> 4 In what ways are the old and the new houses different?
>
> **Look at G.**
>
> 5a Why do you think the garages were built on the High Street, and not in one of the side streets in the village?
>
> 5b Do you think the garages spoil the High Street? Say why, or why not.

Settlements around Newport

Routes and settlements near Newport

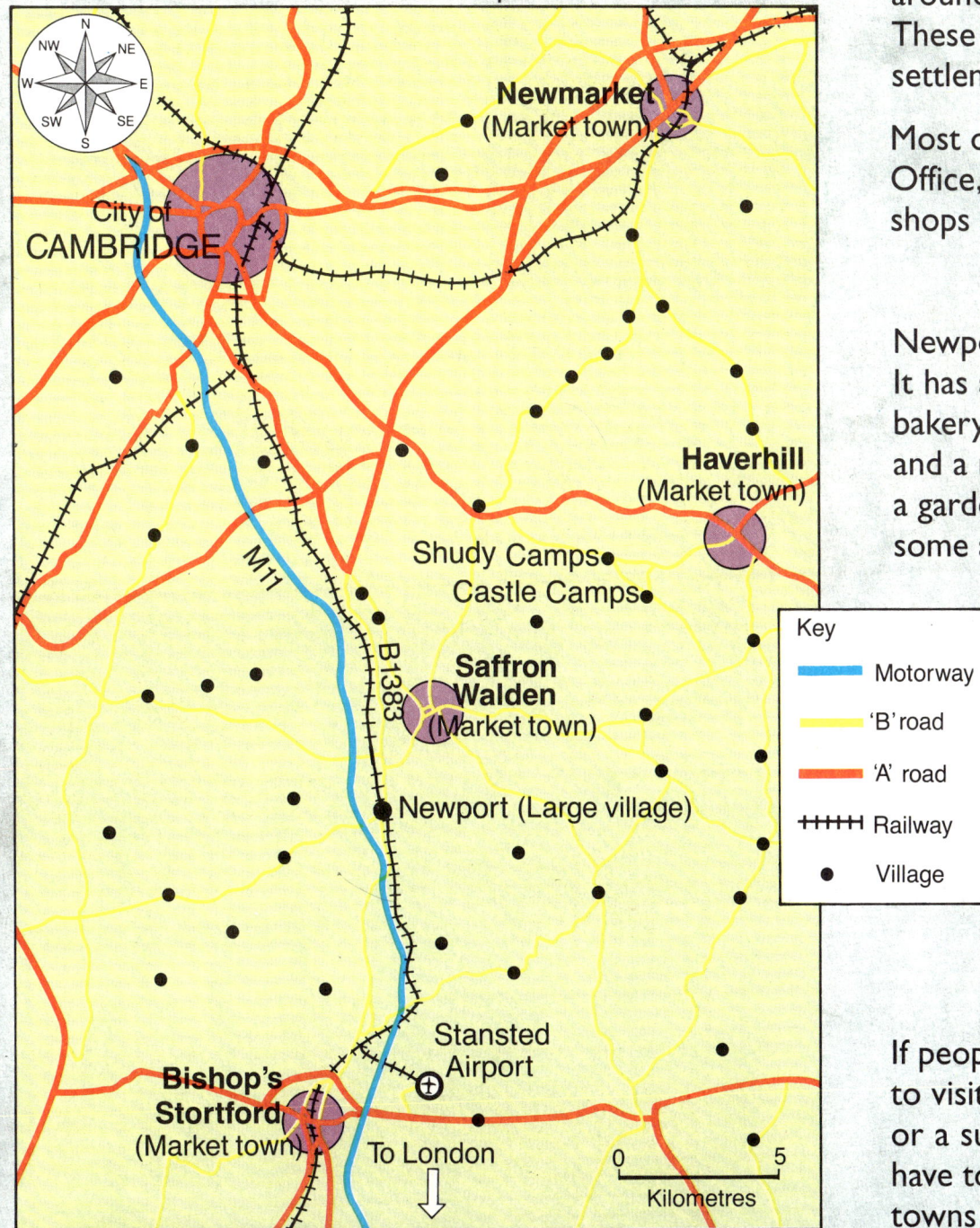

Key	
▬▬▬	Motorway
▬▬▬	'B' road
▬▬▬	'A' road
++++	Railway
●	Village

Map *A* shows the villages and towns in the area around Newport. These places are called settlements.

Most of them have a Post Office, and one or two shops selling food.

Newport is a large village. It has a Post Office, a bakery, a general store (*D*) and a newsagent. It also has a gardening centre and some antique shops.

If people in the villages want to visit an open-air market or a supermarket, they have to travel to one of the towns nearby.

Look at *A*.

1a What is the nearest market town to Newport?

1b Which market town can people from Newport travel to by train?

1c What kind of settlement is there most of on map *A*? Villages, towns or cities? Name one of each.

Saffron Walden and Haverhill are market towns near Newport (see map *A* on page 31). *B* shows the open-air market at Haverhill.

People can buy most things they need in the market towns, but there are not many large shops.

If people in Newport want a choice of large shops, they have to travel to the city of Cambridge (see map *A* on page 31). Here, they can find most of the large chain stores (*C*).

There are several big bookshops (*D*) to choose from in Cambridge, but very few in the nearby market towns.

People can travel to Cambridge by car, bus or train.

The car journey along the M11 is very quick. But it is hard to drive in Cambridge. The streets are narrow and there are few places to park (E).

E

The journey by bus is slower than by car, but there are no parking problems.

Travelling by train is quick but it costs more than the bus journey. Also, the station is not in the city centre.

F

Bus
1 bus every 2 hours
Journey takes 1 hour

NEWPORT → CAMBRIDGE

Train
1 train every hour
Journey takes 37 minutes

Look at B, C and D.

2a B shows the market at Haverhill. What can you buy here that you cannot buy in Newport?

2b What can you buy in the shops in C and D that you cannot buy in Newport?

Look at E and F.

3a Many of the streets in Cambridge are one-way streets. Can you think why?

3b Which way would you choose to travel from Newport to Cambridge? By car, bus or train? Say why.

A French market town: Le Puy

Where is Le Puy?

Le Puy is a town in the mountains of the Central Massif in France (A).

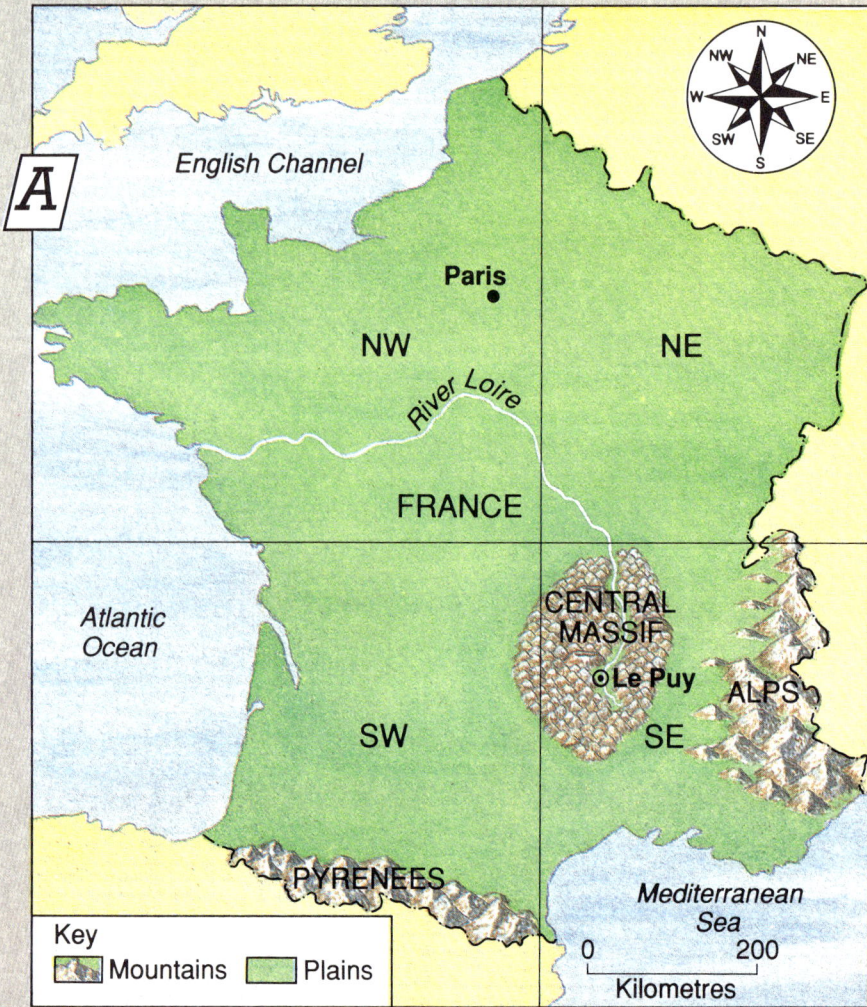

A

English Channel

Paris

NW

NE

River Loire

FRANCE

Atlantic
Ocean

CENTRAL
MASSIF

○Le Puy

ALPS

SW

SE

PYRENEES

Mediterranean
Sea

0   200

Kilometres

Key
Mountains   Plains

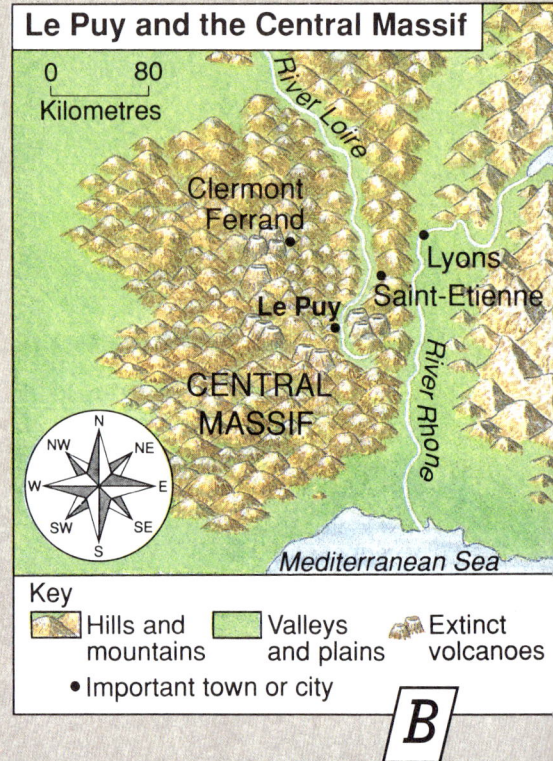

Le Puy and the Central Massif

0   80

Kilometres

River Loire

Clermont
Ferrand

Lyons

Le Puy   Saint-Etienne

CENTRAL
MASSIF

River Rhone

Mediterranean Sea

B

Key
Hills and
mountains
Valleys
and plains
Extinct
volcanoes
● Important town or city

On map *B* of the Central Massif you can see several volcanoes. The volcanoes stopped erupting a very long time ago. They are now extinct. You can see some of the extinct volcanoes in *C*.

C

V V V V
V   V V V
V V V
V

C is a view of Le Puy. Look at the volcanoes in the distance. They are marked with a V.

Maps *A* and *B* tell us that Le Puy is very near the valley of the River Loire. The Loire is one of the main rivers in France.

Map *D* shows that Le Puy is on a tributary of the River Loire. The tributary is called the River Borne. You can see the Borne valley in *E*.

Map *D* also shows that the roads, the railway and the town of Le Puy have been built on the lower land in the valleys.

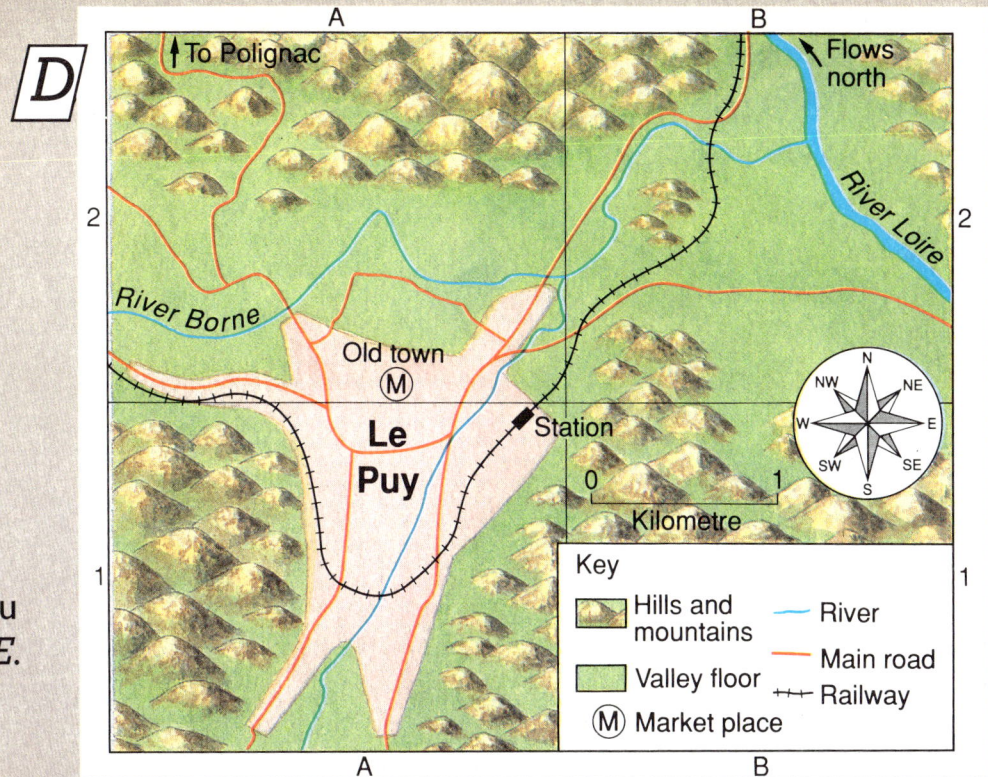

D

To Polignac

Flows north

River Loire

River Borne

Old town
(M)

Le Puy

Station

0   1
Kilometre

Key
Hills and mountains
Valley floor
(M) Market place
— River
— Main road
+++ Railway

E

Look at *A* and *B*.

1a Map *A* is divided into four squares, or quarters. In which quarter of France is Le Puy? North-west, north-east, south-west or south-east?

1b Name three groups of mountains in southern France.

1c What is the nearest sea to Le Puy?

Look at *D* and *E*.

2a Why were the roads and the railway built in the valley and not in the hills?

2b Is the oldest part of Le Puy at the north end or the south end of the town?

3 Write about what you can see in *E*.

What does Le Puy look like?

A is a drawing of Le Puy. The building on the tall rock at the front is a church. It was built 800 years ago. Behind the church is a rock with a statue on it. This is called the Rocher Corneille. Both these tall rocks are the remains of old volcanoes.

B is a view of the oldest part of Le Puy. The Rocher Corneille is in the background.

Le Puy from the north-west

Central Massif

Rocher Corneille

Cathedral

Aiguilhe

Below the Rocher Corneille is the cathedral (C). It is 700 years old. The houses and the narrow streets of the old town were built around the cathedral (D).

Le Puy: the Old Town

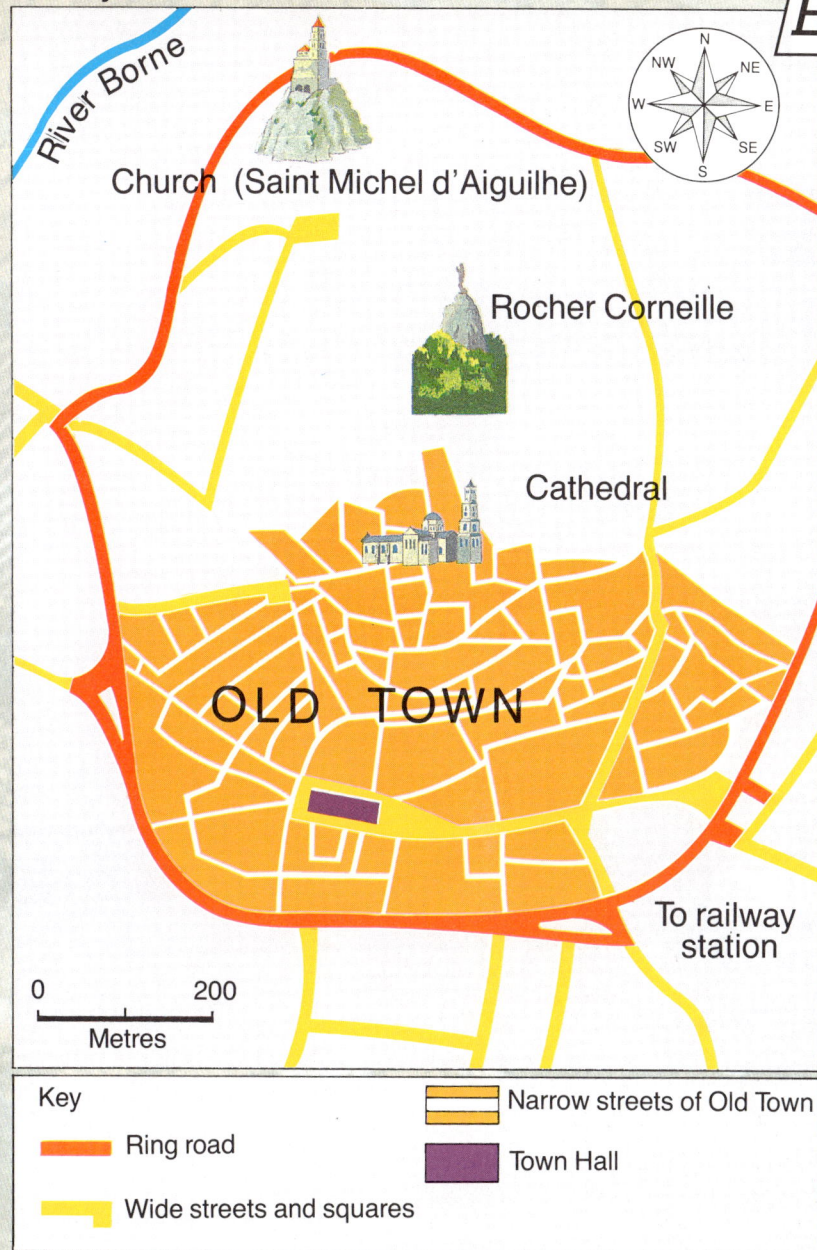

Key

■ Ring road

□ Wide streets and squares

▨ Narrow streets of Old Town

■ Town Hall

Map labels: River Borne · Church (Saint Michel d'Aiguilhe) · Rocher Corneille · Cathedral · OLD TOWN · To railway station · 0 200 Metres · E

You can see the old part of Le Puy on map E. Look at the narrow streets in the centre. A new ring road has been built around the town. You can see it on E.

The newer parts of Le Puy look different from the old town. F is a view of a new part of the town on the north-west side.

F

Look at A.

1a L'aiguille is the French word for needle. Why do you think the church is called Saint Michel d'Aiguilhe?

1b Why do you think the church was built on top of the rock needle?

1c Write about what you can see in A.

Look at C, D, E and F.

2a List the differences between the old and the new parts of Le Puy.

2b Why do you think a ring road was built around Le Puy?

Le Puy the tourist town

Le Puy is a popular tourist town (A). Tourists come to Le Puy to see the rock needles and the beautiful old buildings and narrow streets.

Tourists also come to Le Puy to buy lace. Lace has been made in the town for a very long time. It is sold in shops called Les Dentellières (B). C shows one of the local lace patterns.

"Lace has been made by the women of Le Puy for over 400 years. I was taught to make it by my mother and she was taught by my grandmother. It takes a lot of skill and time to make this lace. That is why it costs a lot to buy."

D tells us what a young woman says about making lace in Le Puy.

Look at A.

1a What can you see in A which tells you that Le Puy is a tourist town?

1b Give three reasons why tourists come to Le Puy.

Look at C and D.

2a Why is lace expensive to buy?

2b Draw your own lace pattern.

Le Puy the market town

Routes and settlements near Le Puy

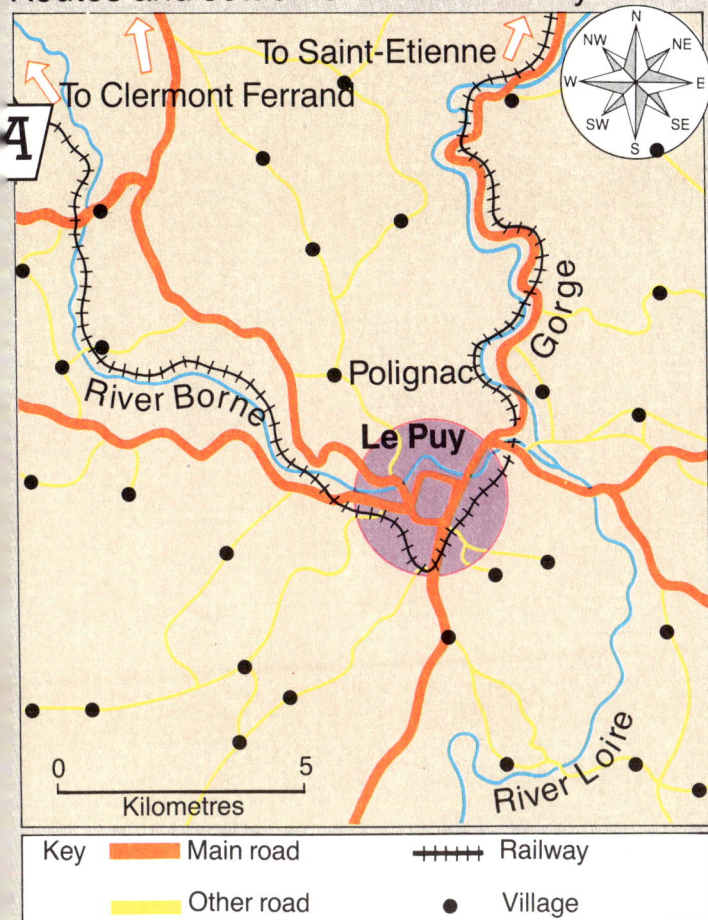

To Saint-Etienne
To Clermont Ferrand
A
Gorge
Polignac
River Borne
Le Puy
River Loire

0 — 5
Kilometres

Key
Main road ━━━ Railway ┼┼┼┼┼
Other road ━━━ Village ●

B

There are many small villages
in the mountains around Le Puy (A).
One village is Polignac (B). The ruins of its
castle stand on the remains of an old volcano.

There are very few shops in
the villages near Le Puy. The
villagers have to travel to
Le Puy for most of the things
they need to buy.

People from the villages travel to
Le Puy by car, bus or train.
C shows the main road and
the railway running through
a narrow part of the Loire valley.
A deep, narrow valley like this
is called a gorge.

C

Look at A and C.

1a How do most people travel to
Le Puy from the nearby villages and
towns? (Look at the routes on A.)

1b Why do people need to go to Le Puy
from the small villages nearby?

Look at C.

2 Make a drawing of C and label
the road, the River Loire, the
railway tunnel and the gorge.

39

Le Puy has many shops and
an open-air market (*D*).
Market day is very busy.
It is the day when people from
nearby villages come into the
town to do their shopping.

The market is held in the
main square of the town.
It is on flat ground next
to the Town Hall, and below
the cathedral.

There has been a market in
Le Puy for hundreds of years.
E is an old photograph which
shows the cattle market
in 1900.

Many market goods are
brought in by farmers from
around the town.
Photographs *F*, *G*, *H* and *I*
show some of the things
they sell.

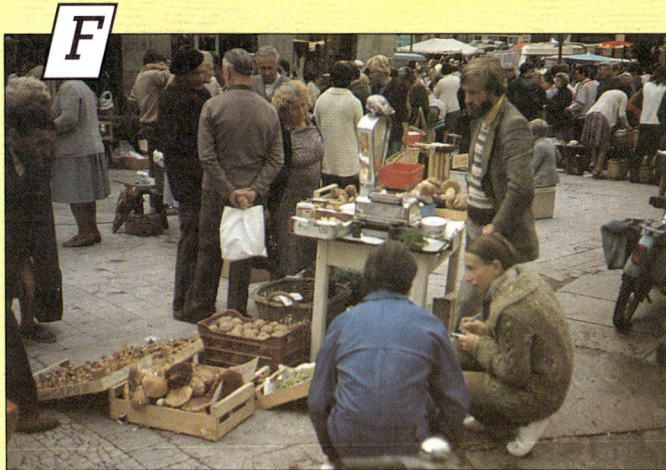

These wild mushrooms are all different shapes, sizes and varieties (F). They are collected from woods and fields in the Central Massif.

Rabbits are another favourite food in this part of France (H).

Live chickens are reared on local farms and brought to the market to sell (G).

Vegetables and fruit are sold on many of the market stalls, and local cheeses too (I)

Look at D and E.

3a What was sold in Le Puy's market in 1900?

3b Write a letter to tell some friends where to find the market square in Le Puy. Use E and map E on page 37 to help you.

Look at D, F, G, H and I.

4a Make a list of the things you can see on sale in the market.

4b What things are sold at Le Puy market that you cannot buy in your local market or supermarket?

Old Delhi

Abe and Amrita Abraham
(A) live in Delhi. It is the
capital city of India.

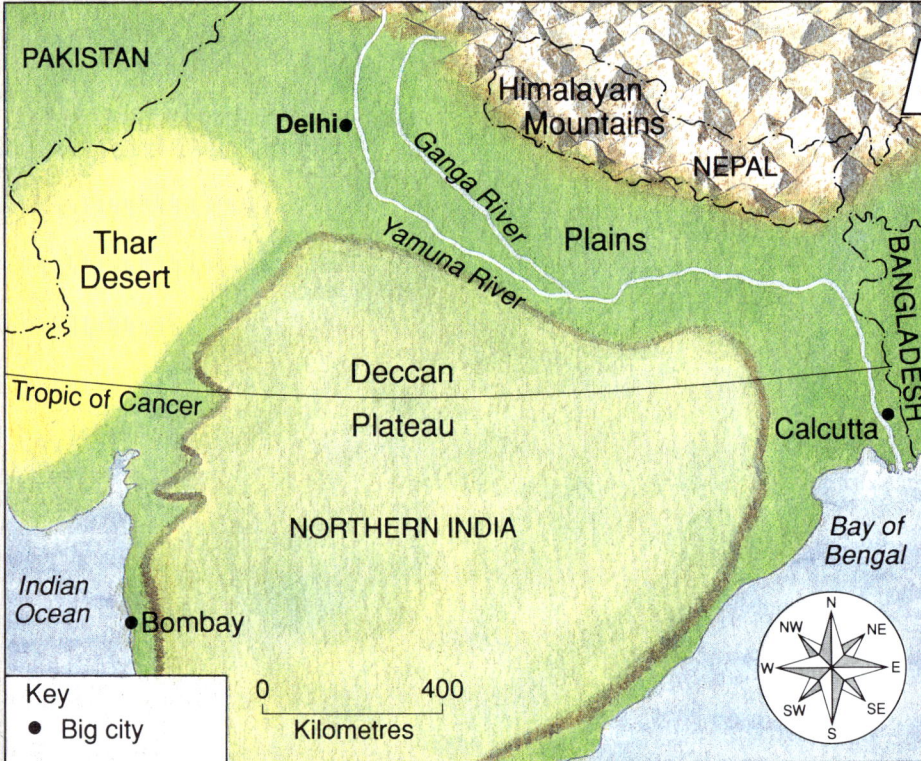

Map B shows that Delhi is
on the River Yamuna, which
joins the River Ganga.

Abe and Amrita Abraham are
journalists. Amrita works for the
Indian Express which is one of
the main English language newspapers
in India (C). Abe works for
the *Sunday Mail*.

D shows people working in
a Delhi newspaper office.

Delhi is divided into two parts, Old Delhi and New Delhi. The *Sunday Mail* office is in New Delhi (map *C* page 48). The offices of the *Indian Express* are on the edge of Old Delhi (*E*). You can see them on map *F*. Map *F* also shows some of the most famous buildings in Old Delhi.

E

Read INDIAN EXPRESS

Old Delhi

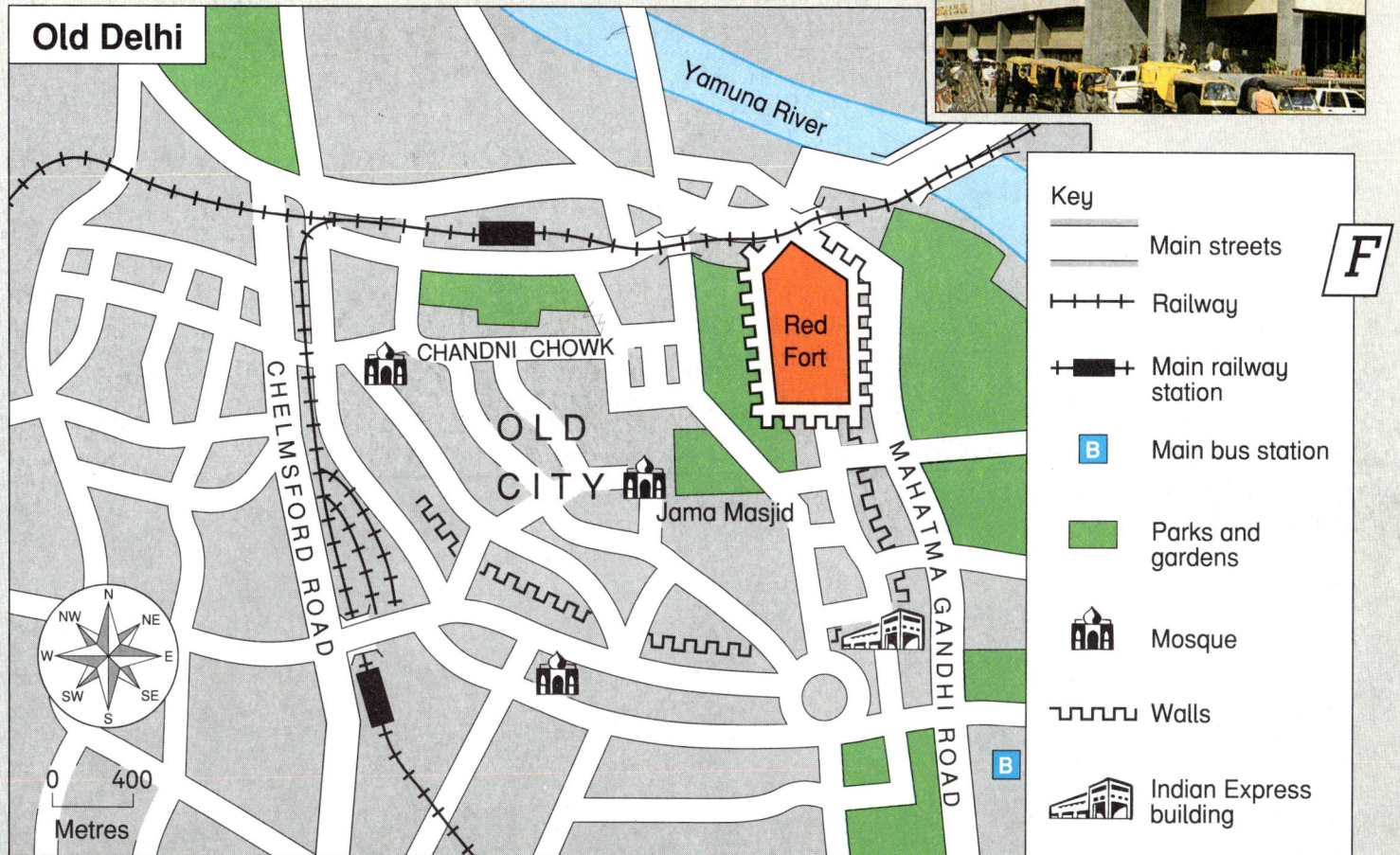

F

Yamuna River

CHANDNI CHOWK

Red Fort

OLD CITY

Jama Masjid

CHELMSFORD ROAD

MAHATMA GANDHI ROAD

NW N NE
W E
SW S SE

0   400
Metres

Key

Main streets

Railway

Main railway station

B Main bus station

Parks and gardens

Mosque

Walls

Indian Express building

B

Look at *B*.

1 Name the country which is:
a) west of Delhi,
b) east of Calcutta,
c) where you find the Himalayas.

2 Name:
a) the sea that the River Ganga runs into,
b) three cities in India.

Look at *F*.

3a Is Amrita Abraham's office north or south of Red Fort?

3b In which two directions does the railway run between the River Yamuna and the station in Chelmsford Road?

3c In what direction is the Jama Masjid mosque from the Red Fort?

A neighbourhood in Old Delhi

More than 8 million people live in Delhi. The streets are always full of traffic and people. The main street in Old Delhi is called Chandni Chowk (A).

There are open-air markets in many of the streets of Old Delhi. They are called bazaars. B, C and D show some of the things that are sold in the bazaars.

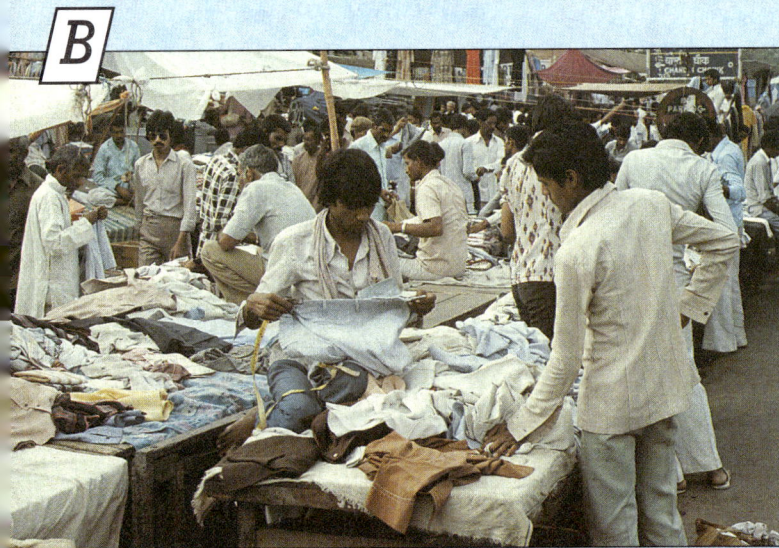

At the eastern end of Chandni Chowk is one of the oldest buildings in Delhi. It is called the Red Fort (*E*). It was built hundreds of years ago to defend the city.

South of Chandni Chowk is the Jama Masjid mosque (*F*). A mosque is a building where Muslims worship. This mosque is one of the largest in India.

G is a view across Old Delhi from the top of the Jama Masjid mosque.

Look at *B*, *C* and *D*.

1a Make a list of some things on sale in the bazaar.

1b In what ways is Chandni Chowk different from a main street in a British city?

Look at *G*.

2 Write about what you can see in the photograph.

Public transport is cheaper in India than in Britain, but the poorest people cannot afford to use it.

People travel around Delhi in many different forms of transport.
Cars mix with bullock carts (*H*) and the buses are often bursting at the doors (*I*).

Some people can afford to buy motor bikes (*J*). Motor bikes are also used as taxis (*K*), and there are bicycle rickshaws for hire as well (*L*).

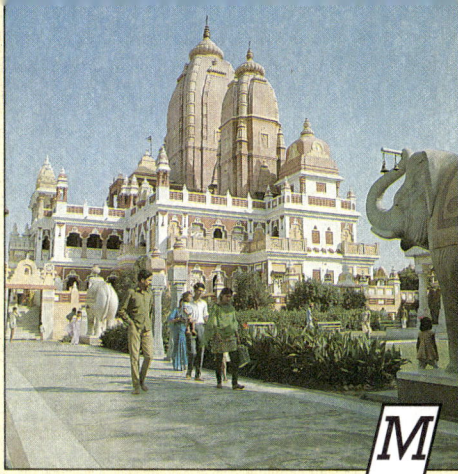

The main religion of India is Hinduism. *M* shows the largest Hindu temple in Delhi.

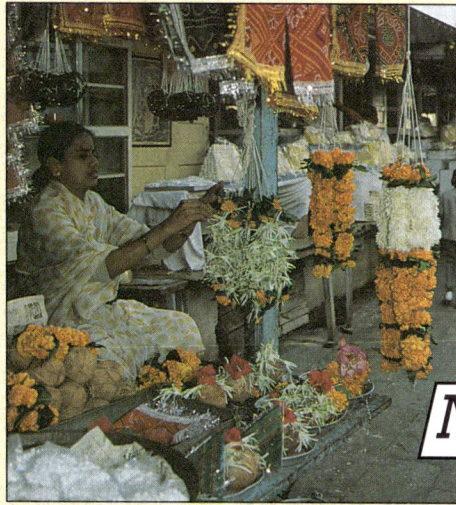

Garlands of flowers are often worn at Hindu festivals (*N*).

One of the main Hindu festivals is called Dessehra. It lasts for ten days and is a time when Hindus worship the goddess Durga (*O*).

Ravana   Durga

Plays are acted in the streets during Dessehra. *P* shows statues of Ravana, who was an evil king in the Hindu story of Rama.

Look at *H, I, J, K* and *L.*

3a The photographs show different forms of transport. Make a list of them all, starting with the slowest, and ending with the fastest.

3b Choose one of the vehicles shown in the photographs and describe a journey on or in it through Old Delhi.

Look at *M*, and at *F* on page 45.

4 What sort of buildings are mosques and temples? Who worships in them?

Look at *P.*

5a Name a festival that is held in Britain on 5 November. Find out about the story of the festival.

5b Find and read the Hindu story of Rama.

A neighbourhood in New Delhi

When Delhi became the capital city of India, a new city was built to the south-west of Old Delhi. This new part is called New Delhi. It is a planned city, with many wide, tree-lined streets and parks (A).

The sign in B is in English and in Hindi. Hindi is the language that most people speak.

C is a map of a small part of New Delhi. The area is called Connaught Place. The streets have been built in circles and in straight lines.

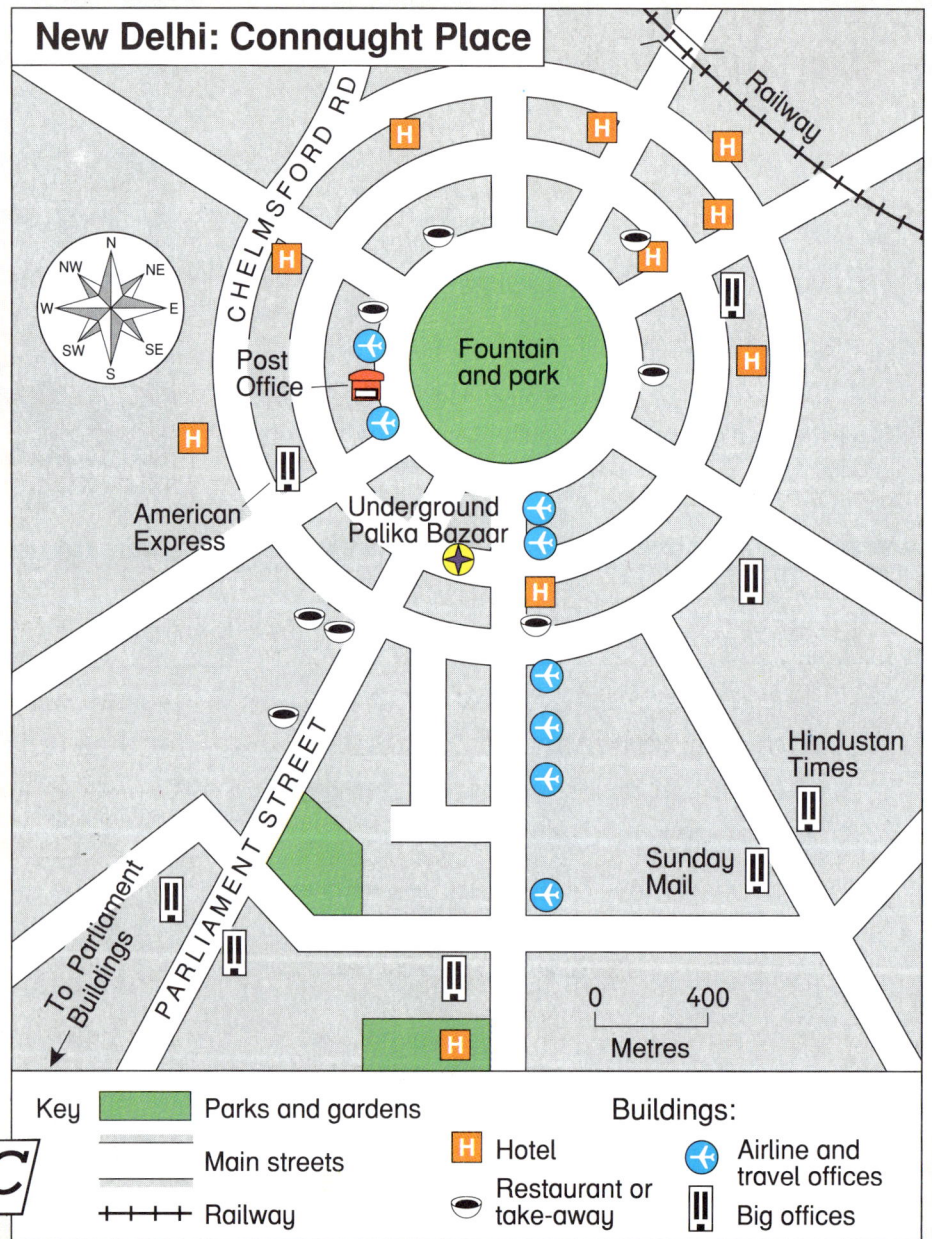

New Delhi: Connaught Place

CHELMSFORD RD

Railway

Post Office

Fountain and park

American Express

Underground Palika Bazaar

Hindustan Times

Sunday Mail

To Parliament Buildings

PARLIAMENT STREET

0   400
Metres

Key

Parks and gardens

Main streets

Railway

Buildings:

H Hotel

Restaurant or take-away

Airline and travel offices

Big offices

D

The main office buildings are near Connaught Place. The huge new bank in *D* is one of them. You can see street traders next to the bank. They sell their goods to the office workers.

E

Not far from Connaught Place are the Indian government buildings (*E*).

F

The wide road in *F* is where a Republican Day Parade is held every year. It celebrates the time when India became independent in 1947. Before 1947, India was part of the British Empire.

Look at *C*.

1a Name three types of building that are found around Connaught Place.

1b Which newspaper offices are in the area shown on map *C*?

1c Write about a walk in New Delhi, from the Post Office to the hotel in the park. Say what buildings you pass, and in which direction you walk.

Look at *C*, and at map *F* on page 43.

2 Name three types of building near Chandni Chowk that are *not* found near Connaught Place.

3 Which part of Delhi would you like to visit most? Say why.

Rich and poor in Delhi

Housing in Delhi

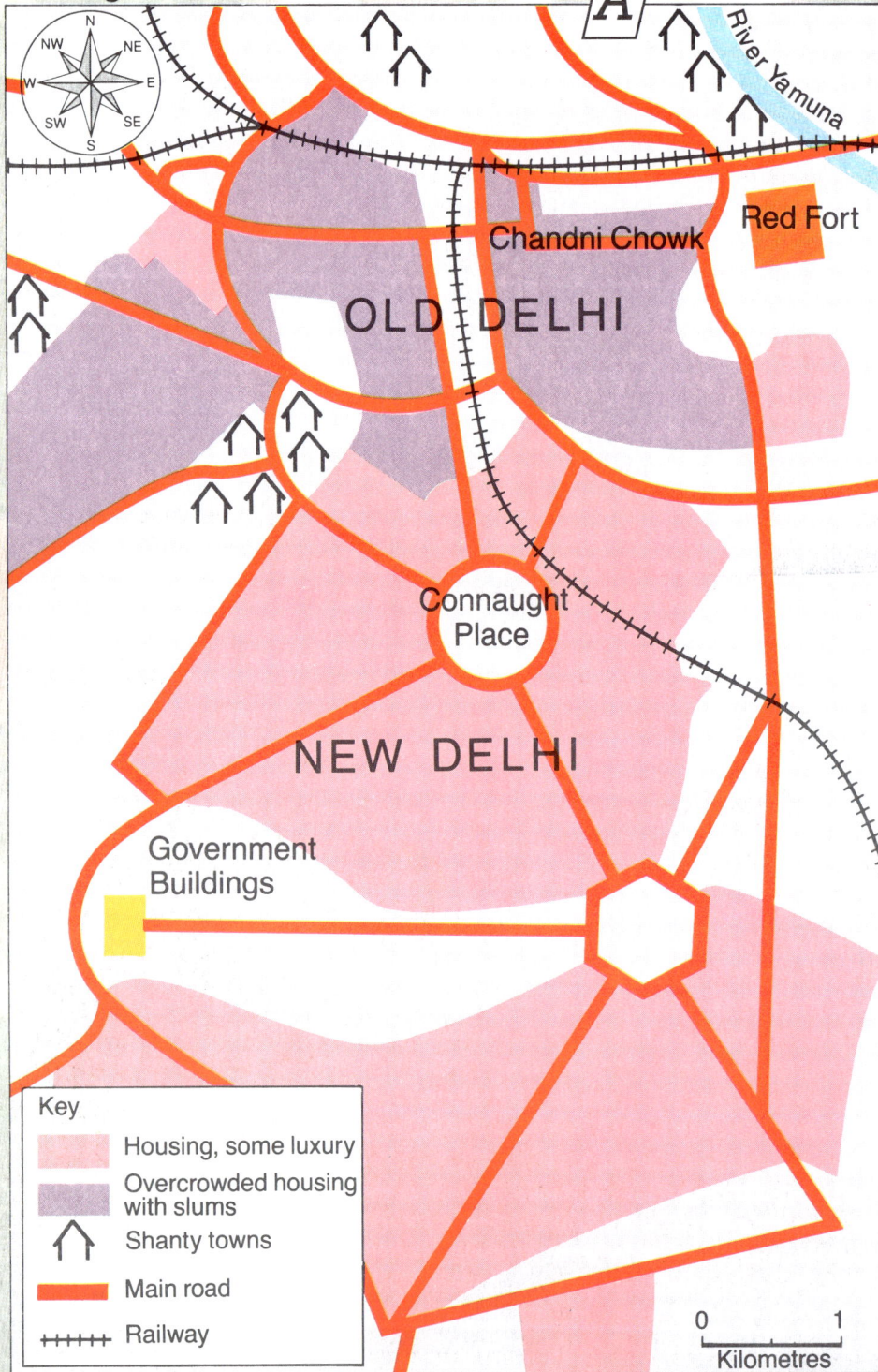

A

OLD DELHI

Chandni Chowk

Red Fort

River Yamuna

Connaught Place

NEW DELHI

Government Buildings

Key
- Housing, some luxury
- Overcrowded housing with slums
- Shanty towns
- Main road
- Railway

0   1
Kilometres

Delhi, like many big cities, has different sorts of housing. Map *A* shows that most of the overcrowded housing is in Old Delhi.

Millions of people live here (*B*) Many families have only one room. These are not the poorest people.

B

The very poor people live in shanty towns around the edge of Old Delhi (*A* and *C*). Three million people live in these shanty towns.

C

The shanty dwellers earn their living on the streets of the city. The man in *D* collects old newspapers from houses in the wealthiest parts of Delhi.

E shows a street stall where food is sold to people as they pass by. Many of the poorer people make and sell food like this.

For tourists to Delhi, and for people who have well-paid jobs, there are good restaurants to eat in (*F*). In New Delhi, there are also several grand hotels(*G*).

Look at *A*.

1a In which part of Delhi do most people live?

1b In which part of Delhi would you find the largest homes? Why?

1c Choose one of the shanty towns on the map.
In which part of the city is it?
Write about the shanty town.

The weather in Delhi

Look at the weather graphs in *A*. The graphs can only tell us what the weather is like on *most* days in a month. Some days, it may be cooler or hotter than the temperatures shown on the graphs.

A

Climate: Delhi

Months	J	F	M	A	M	J	J	A	S	O	N	D	
Temperatures in degrees C	14	18	23	30	33	34	30	29	28	25	20	15	
Millimetres of rainfall	25	22	17	7	8	65	211	173	150	31	1	5	Total 715

Climate: London

Months	J	F	M	A	M	J	J	A	S	O	N	D	
Temperatures in degrees C	4	4	6	8	12	15	17	16	14	10	7	5	
Millimetres of rainfall	48	43	46	38	46	51	61	56	46	66	61	61	Total 623

Key: Wet · Dry · Very hot · Hot · Warm · Mild or cool

Look at the two weather forecasts for different days in the year (*B*). Compare the temperatures shown in *B* with the ones for the same months in *A*.

B shows that the weather in summer is usually very hot. This is what Amrita says about the winter weather (*C*).

Weather forecast for Dehli
January 7th

Weather

Forecast for Thursday: Mist or fog in the morning. Mainly clear sky.
The highest temperature on Wednesday was 24.4 degrees C and the lowest temperature was 9.3 degrees C.

B June 4th

Weather

Forecast for Saturday: Mainly clear sky. Thunder possible in some areas during evening or night. Not much change in day temperature.
The highest temperature on Friday was 41.7 degrees C and the lowest temperature was 31.1 degrees C.

"In December and January, night temperatures can go as low as two degrees for several days. Day temperatures can be twelve degrees. This seems cold for us tropical people. Abe goes to work in a sweater and I wear a shawl (*D*)."

C

D

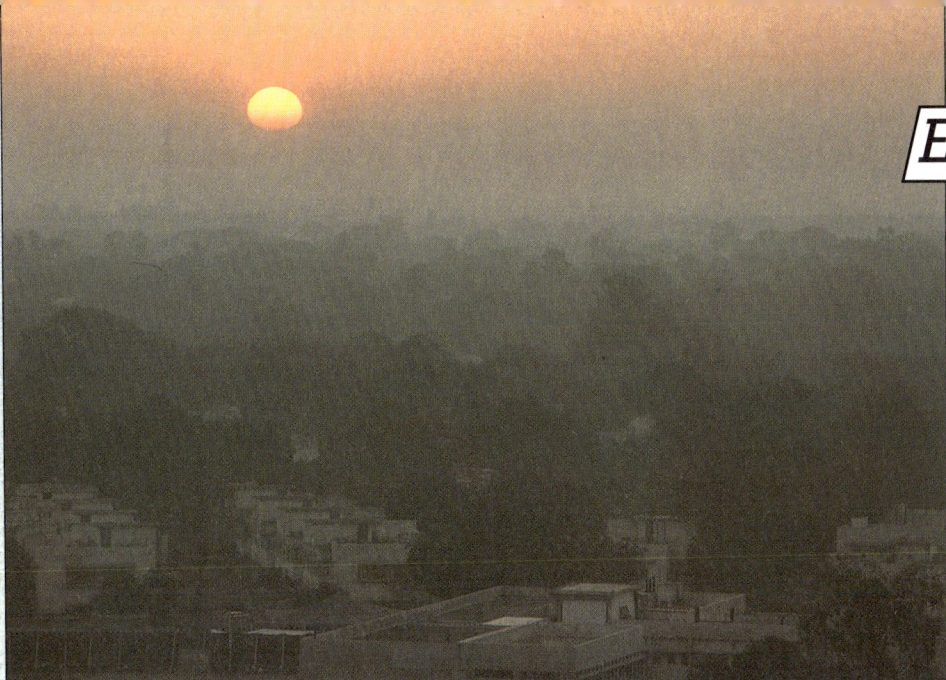
E

Fogs and smogs often happen in Delhi. This is because the air is often damp, and it is smoky and dirty. You can see smog over the city in *E*.

F

There are four months in the year when Delhi can be very wet. This is called the monsoon season (*A*). Sometimes it rains so heavily that the city streets are soon flooded (*F*).

Look at *A* and *B*.

1a   How many millimetres of rain fall in the wet monsoon season in Delhi?

1b   Which is the wettest season of the year in London?

1c   Name the hottest, coolest, driest and wettest months in both cities.

1d   If you went to Delhi on holiday in July, what clothes would you pack in your suitcase? Say why.

53

The Panama Canal

Making a long journey shorter

Map *A* shows two routes that a ship can take to travel from New York to San Francisco. Before the year 1914 all ships had to take the long route, round the southern tip of South America.

The voyage took more than three months, and parts of it were dangerous.
At Cape Horn (*B*), strong winds blow all the time and the sea is often very rough.

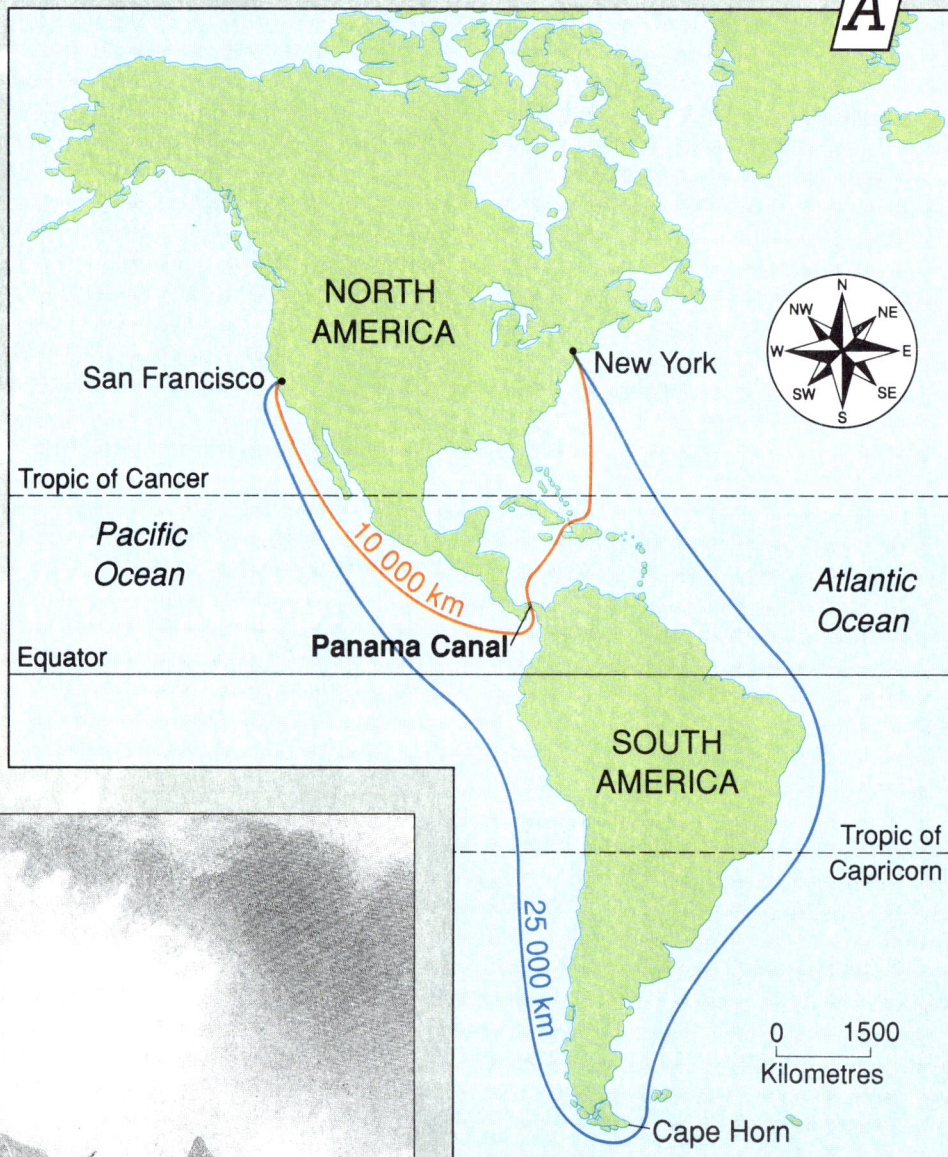

NORTH AMERICA

San Francisco

New York

Tropic of Cancer

Pacific Ocean

10 000 km

Panama Canal

Atlantic Ocean

Equator

SOUTH AMERICA

Tropic of Capricorn

25 000 km

0   1500
Kilometres

Cape Horn

Between 1904 and 1914, a canal was built across the narrow strip of land between North and South America (*C*). Ships could now sail through the canal instead of round Cape Horn.

The canal cut the time of the journey from more than three months to less than one month.

A narrow strip of land between two seas is called an **isthmus**. The Panama isthmus is only 82 kilometres wide at its narrowest point. This is where the Panama Canal was built (*C*).

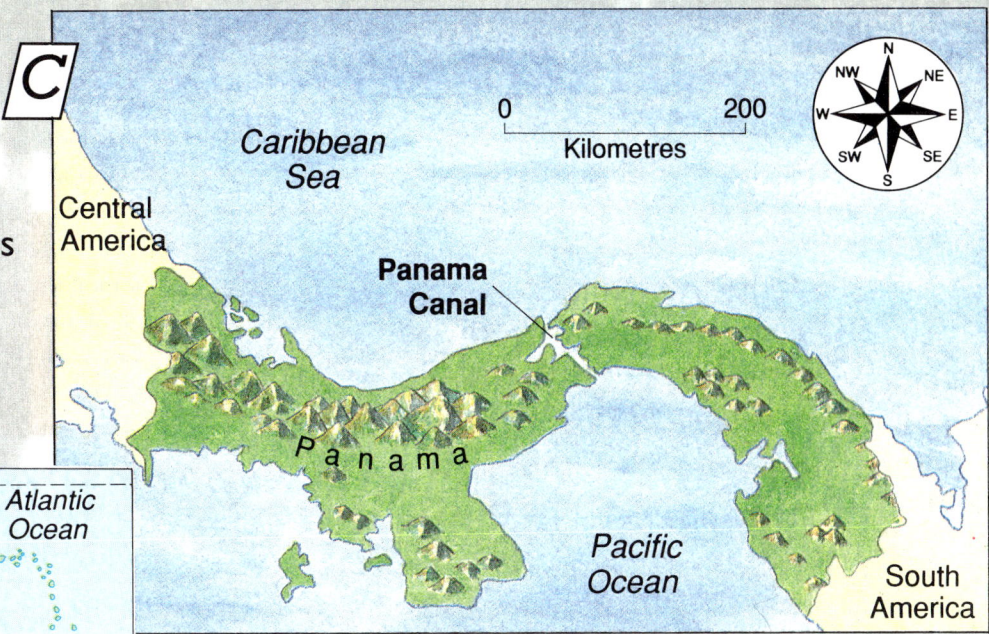

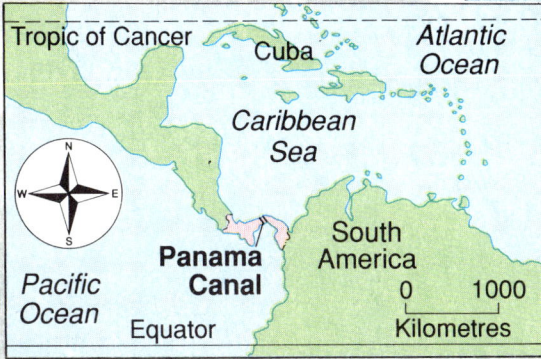

C

Caribbean Sea

Central America

Panama Canal

P a n a m a

Pacific Ocean

South America

0 — 200 Kilometres

Tropic of Cancer

Cuba

Atlantic Ocean

Caribbean Sea

South America

Pacific Ocean

Panama Canal

Equator

0 — 1000 Kilometres

The canal route crosses mountains and lakes. Ships could sail through the lakes, but cuttings had to be made through the mountains. The deepest cutting is called the Gaillard Cut. *D* shows people working on the Cut in 1913.

D

Look at *A*.

1a Which two oceans are linked by the Panama Canal?

1b How many kilometres has the Panama Canal cut off the journey between New York and San Francisco?

Look at *C*.

2 Why was the Panama Canal built where it was?

Look at *D*.

3 Why do you think it took so long to build the Panama Canal?

A journey through the Panama Canal

Let us follow the journey of a ship called *Manhattan* as it travels through the Panama Canal. The route of the journey across Panama is shown on map *A*. It starts at Balboa in the south.

You can see a slice, or section, through the canal journey on *C*.

The *Manhattan* is a huge container ship. Soon after it leaves Balboa, it arrives at the Miraflores locks (*A* and *B*).

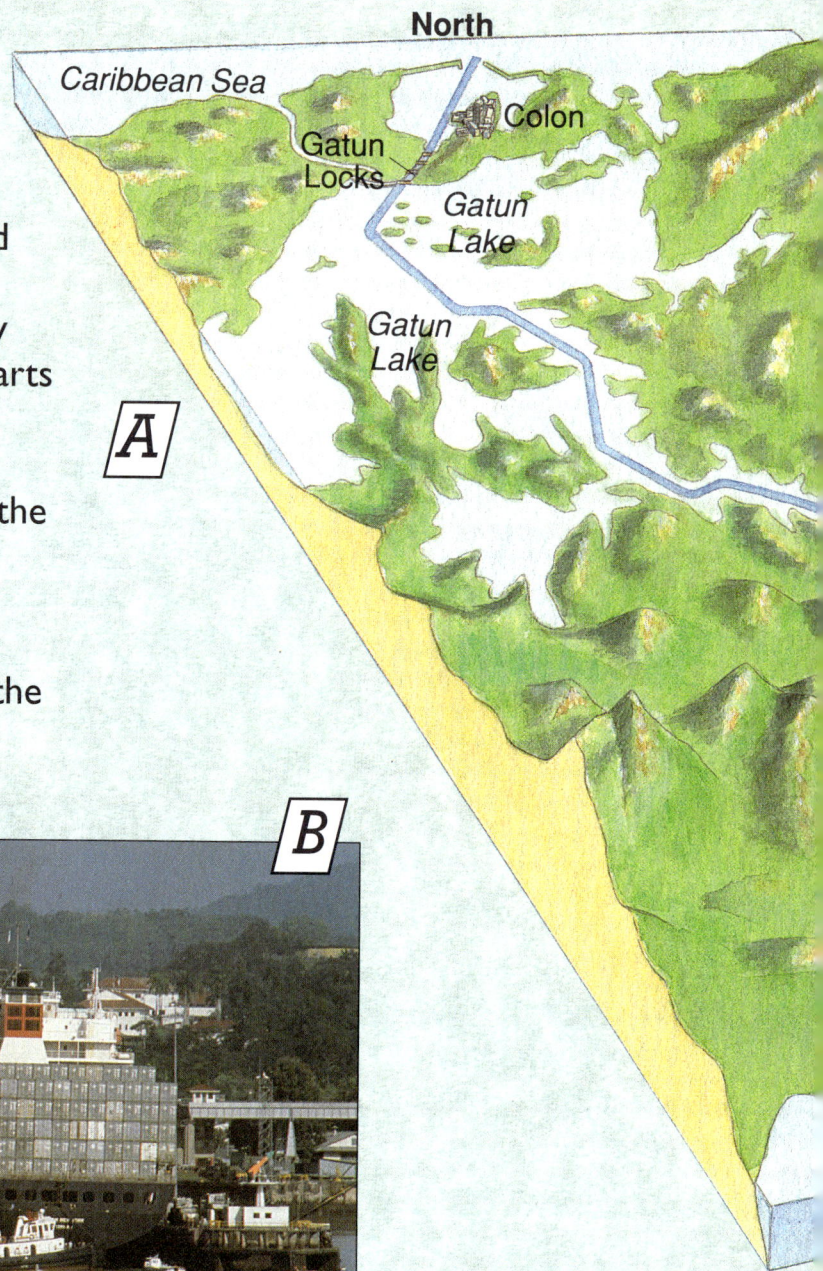

North

Caribbean Sea

Colon

Gatun Locks

Gatun Lake

Gatun Lake

A

B

The locks raise the level of the canal water to the same height as the inland lakes (*C*).

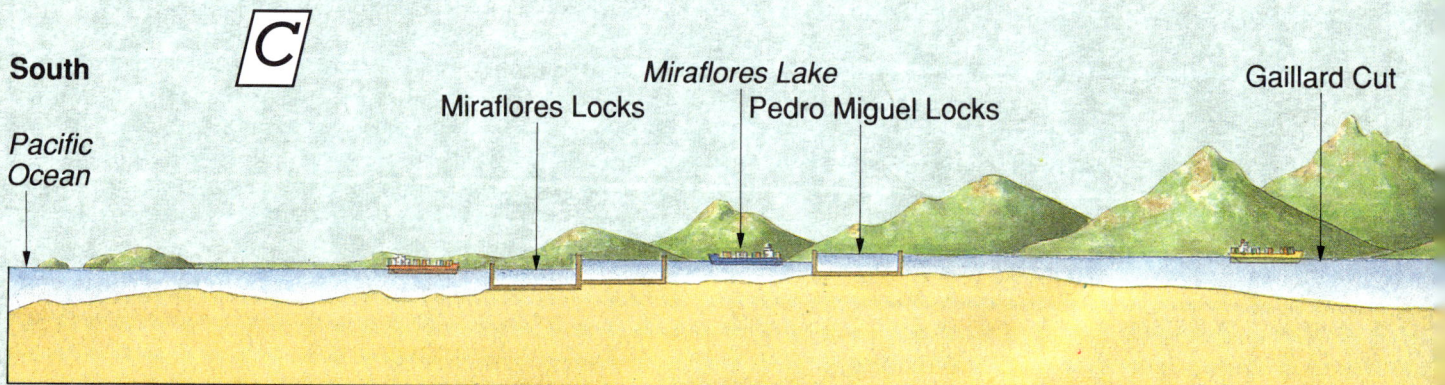

C

South

Miraflores Lake

Miraflores Locks

Pedro Miguel Locks

Gaillard Cut

Pacific Ocean

After leaving the Miraflores locks, the *Manhattan* sails through Miraflores Lake to the next set of locks (*D*). Find these locks on *A* and *C*.

Gaillard Cut

Pedro Miguel Locks

Miraflores Lake

Miraflores Locks

Balboa

Pacific Ocean

South

Key — Panama Canal

Big ships like the *Manhattan* need help to pass in and out of the narrow locks. Small pilot boats (*E*) help to guide them through.

Look at *A* and *C*.

1a Name the town at the northern end of the canal.

1b Name the set of locks which the *Manhattan* went through after Miraflores Lake.

1c Why were locks built on the canal?

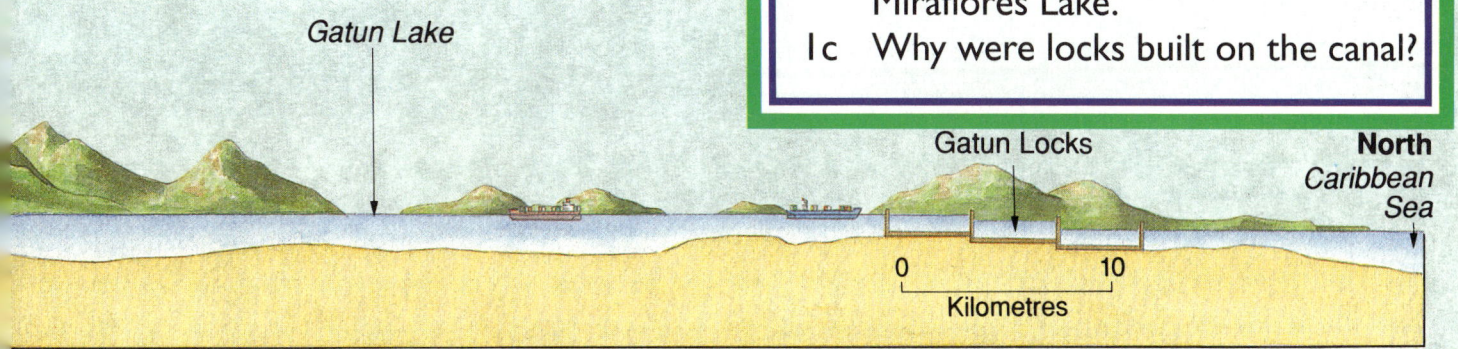

Gatun Lake

Gatun Locks

North
Caribbean Sea

0   10
Kilometres

When the *Manhattan* comes out of the Pedro Miguel locks, it is 25 metres higher than the level of the Pacific Ocean.

Soon after the locks, the *Manhattan* comes to a deep, narrow cutting in the mountains called the Gaillard Cut (*F*). It has to go very slowly here.

F

G

On the other side of the Cut, the canal becomes wider and the *Manhattan* can pass the aircraft carrier (*G*).
The canal then opens out into Gatun Lake. The lake is long and wide so the *Manhattan* can travel faster now.

At the north end of Gatun Lake, there are three more locks. These are called the Gatun locks. Here, the ship is lowered 25 metres to the level of the Caribbean Sea

H

I

Look at the ship. It is in Gatun Lake at the top of the Gatun Locks.

The *Manhattan* will be lowered through the Gatun Locks to the level of the Caribbean Sea (*I*).

J

K

J shows the *Manhattan* in the Gatun locks. It is a tight fit!

The ship has to be pulled through the narrow locks by a small train called a mule (*K*). You can see the railway tracks in *H*.

Look at *H* to *K*.

2a What is needed to help the *Manhattan* get through the Gatun locks? Why?

2b How many locks are there at the end of Gatun Lake? Why are they needed?

Look at pages 56-58.

3 Name the places the *Manhattan* went through along the canal.

4 Which part of the *Manhattan*'s journey was the fastest? Why?

5 Which part of the journey do you think was the slowest? Why?

From London to Lima

Meg and Jim Todd are
going on holiday to Peru.
They want to visit the
ancient ruined city of
Machu Picchu in the
Andes mountains.

They visit a travel agent to
plan their holiday (*A*).
B shows the brochure the
travel agent gives them.

Meg and Jim decide to fly from London to
Lima. Lima is the capital city of Peru (*C*).
The flight to Lima will take over
11 hours (*D*).

Arctic Circle

London

Europe

North America

NORTH ATLANTIC OCEAN

Flight time: 11 hours

Tropic of Cancer

Africa

Equator

Lima

PERU

South America

Tropic of Capricorn

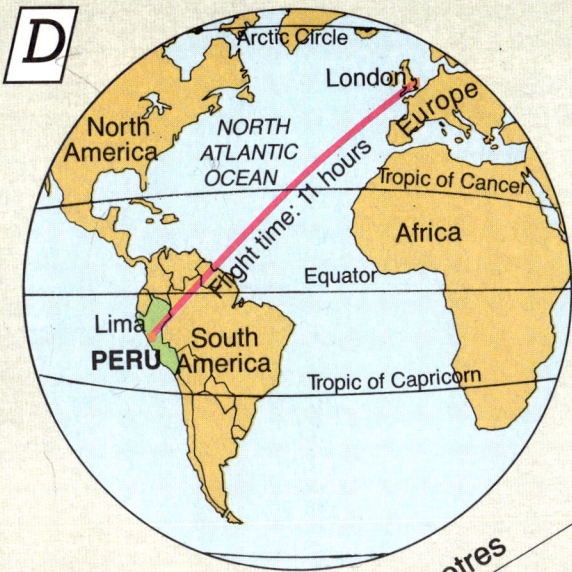

Peru is a mountainous country on the west side of South America (D). Lima is on the flat plain between the coast and the Andes mountains (E).

Andes Mountains

La Oroya   Huancayo

130 kilometres

Valley

E

Coastal Plain

Pacific Ocean   Lima

Key
~~~~ Route of railway

When Meg and Jim arrive in Lima, they will travel on the railway shown in E. This will take them through a steep valley to the town of La Oroya, high up in the Andes mountains.

Look at D.

1a Which ocean does the plane cross on the flight from London to Lima?

1b Which of these does the plane cross over on the flight from London to Lima?

The Arctic Circle   The Tropic of Cancer
The Tropic of Capricorn   The Equator

1c Is Lima north or south of the Equator?

Look at C and E.

2   Write about what you would see around you if you visited Lima.

From Lima to Cuzco

A

Place	Time	Distance in kilometres
LIMA depart	07.40	
LA OROYA arrive	13.40	130
HUANCAYO arrive	16.40	330

Meg and Jim arrive in Lima in the evening.
The next morning, they set off on the
railway journey to La Oroya (A and C).

First, the train crosses the flat coastal plain.
Then it begins to climb up through a valley,
deep in the Andes mountains (B).

The journey is slow because the railway
has to climb up a long way and the slopes
are often very steep.

B

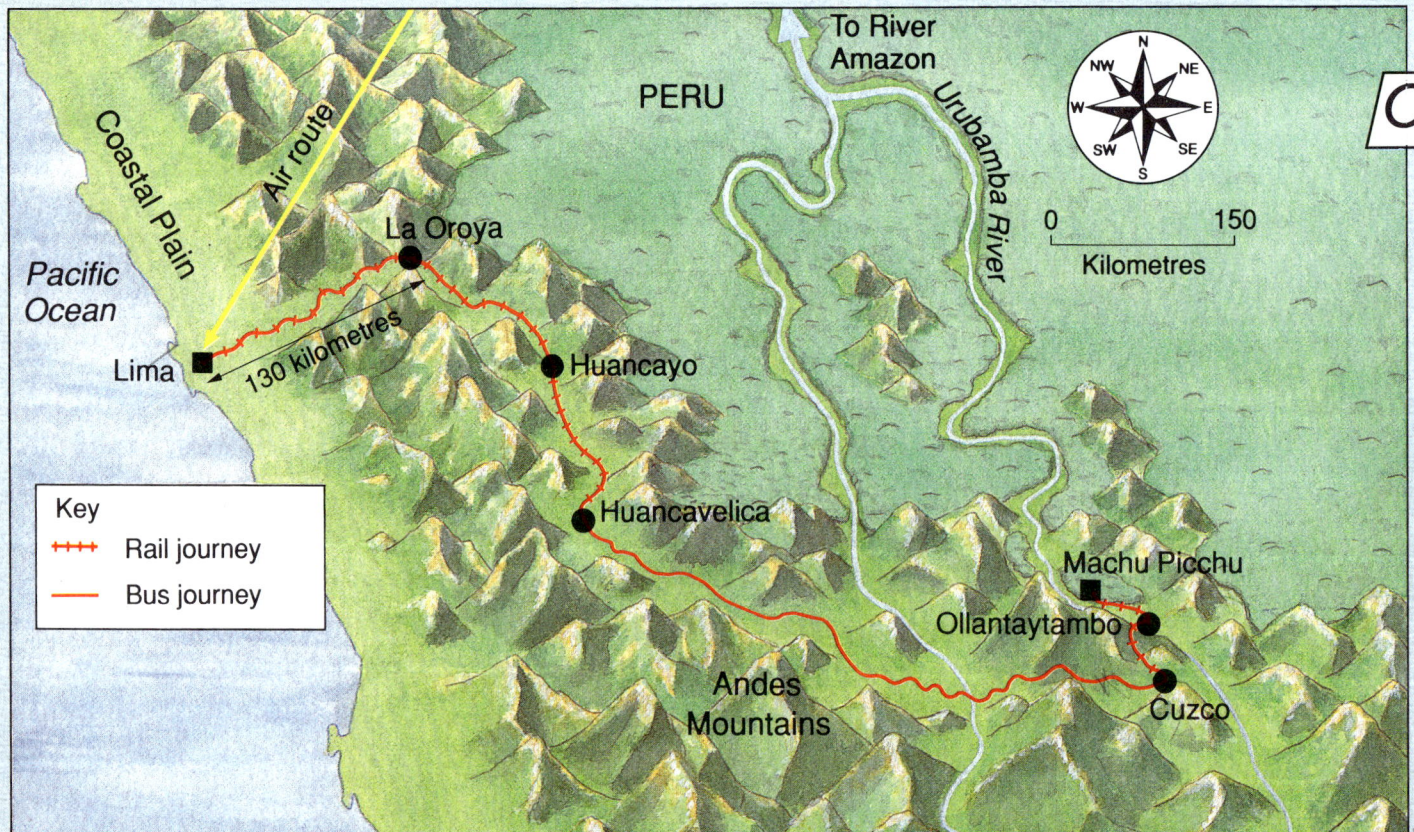

C

Tunnel

Viaduct

Y junction

Road

Railway

D

The railway builders had to build 66 tunnels and 59 viaducts (D) to take the railway up through the mountains. Special Y-shaped junctions had to be made too.

E

The Y junctions are places where the trains zig-zag up the steep slopes, going backwards and forwards (E).

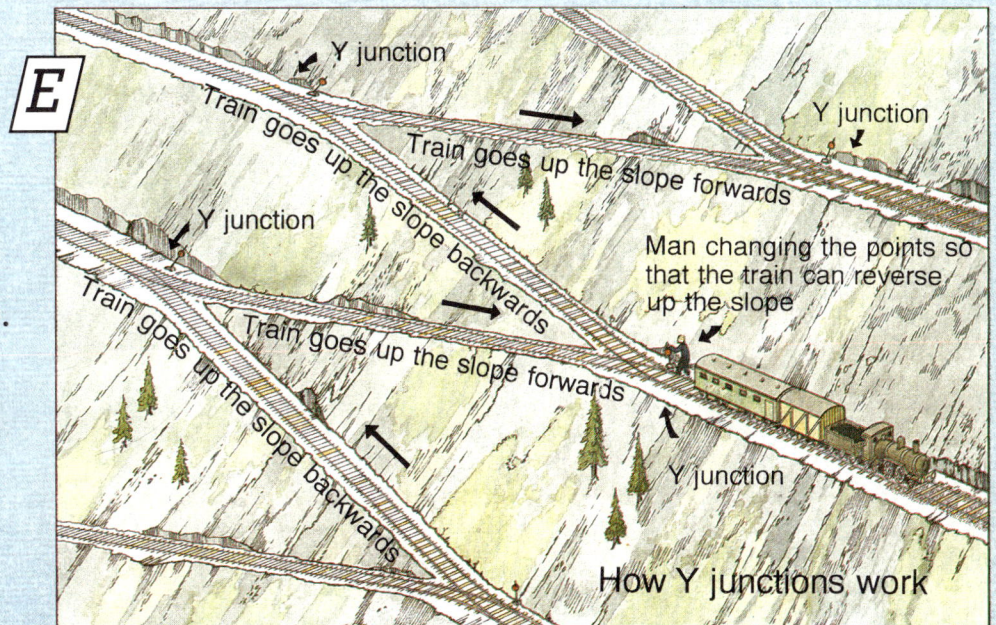

Y junction

Train goes up the slope forwards

Train goes up the slope forwards

Y junction

Y junction

Train goes up the slope backwards

Man changing the points so that the train can reverse up the slope

Train goes up the slope forwards

Train goes up the slope backwards

Y junction

How Y junctions work

Look at A.	Look at B, D and E.
1a How far is it from Lima to Huancayo?	3a What different things did the railway builders do to build the railway up the steep mountain slopes?
1b Which part of the journey takes the most time? How many hours does it take?	
2 Why is the journey from Lima to La Oroya so slow?	3b Draw a picture of a valley in the Andes. Label the railway, the river, a tunnel and a viaduct.

Meg and Jim arrive at Huancayo station in the late afternoon. The town is over 3000 metres high. At this height, there is less oxygen in the air and visitors often feel dizzy and sick (F).

"The sick feeling began when the train arrived in Huancayo. We felt dizzy too and had to lie down at the hotel!"

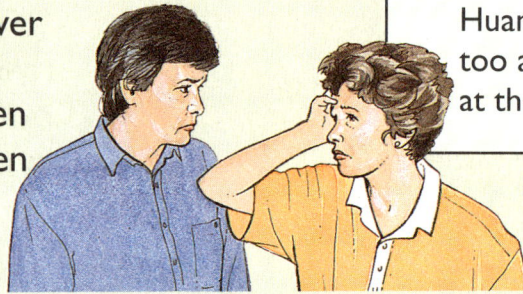

Meg and Jim drink some local tea which makes them feel better. They go for a walk round the market (G and H).

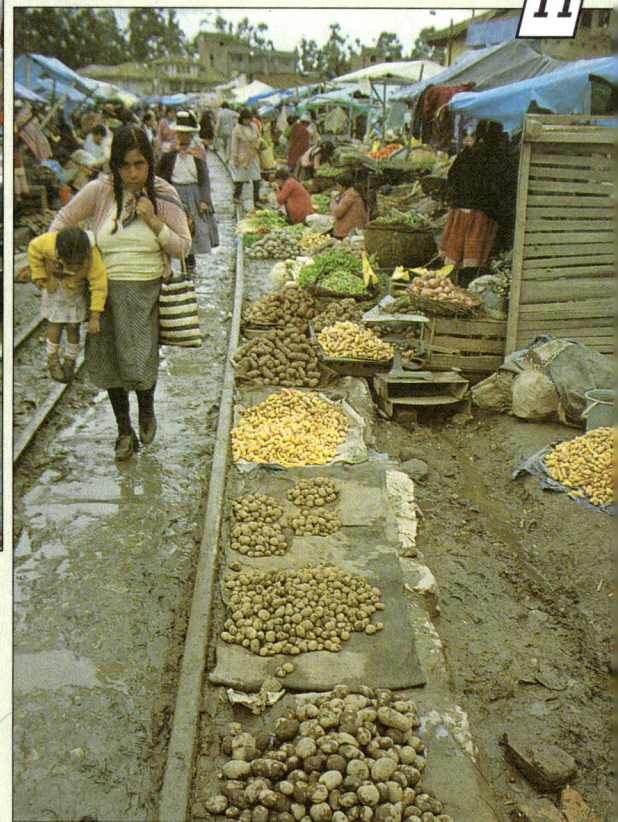

The next day, Meg and Jim catch a steam train to take them to Huancavelica (I and J).

Place	Time	Distance in kilometres
HUANCAYO depart	07.00	
HUANCAVELICA arrive	10.10	130

J

At Huancavelica, the railway line stops.

K

From here to Cuzco, Meg and Jim travel by bus (K). The road is rough and steep, so the journey takes more than three days.

L

They are very tired when they reach Cuzco (L).

Look at *G* and *H*.

4 Write about what you can see in the photographs.

Look at *J* and *K*.

5 How did Meg and Jim travel from Huancayo to Huancavelica, and from Huancavelica to Cuzco?

6 Which part of the journey from Huancayo to Cuzco took the longest? Why?

7 Write the story of Meg and Jim's journey from Huancayo to Cuzco.

From Cuzco to Machu Picchu

A

Cuzco is a very old city. It was once the capital of the empire of the Inca people. The Inca empire was conquered by the Spaniards nearly 400 years ago.

There are still some walls (A) and buildings in Cuzco that were built by the Incas.

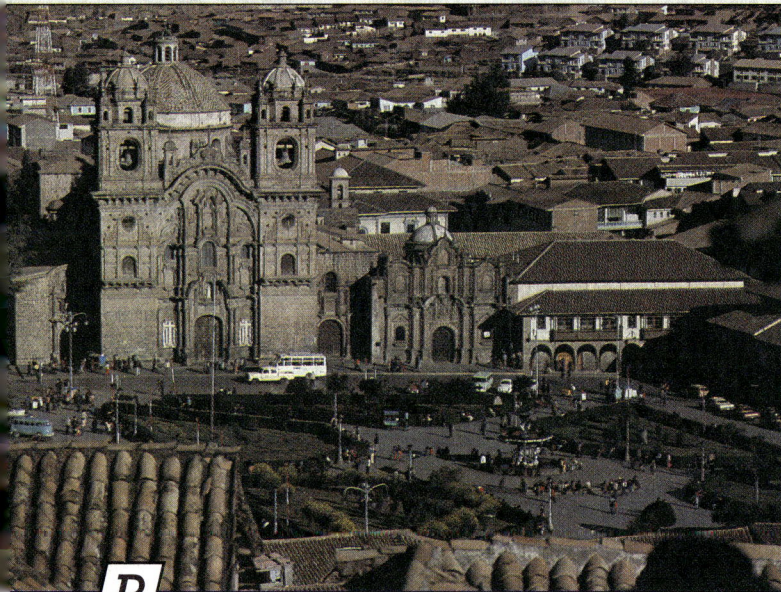

B

Meg and Jim spend the day in the city visiting places such as the cathedral and the square shown in B.

In the morning they set off early on the train journey to Machu Picchu. The first stop is at Ollantaytambo (C).

C

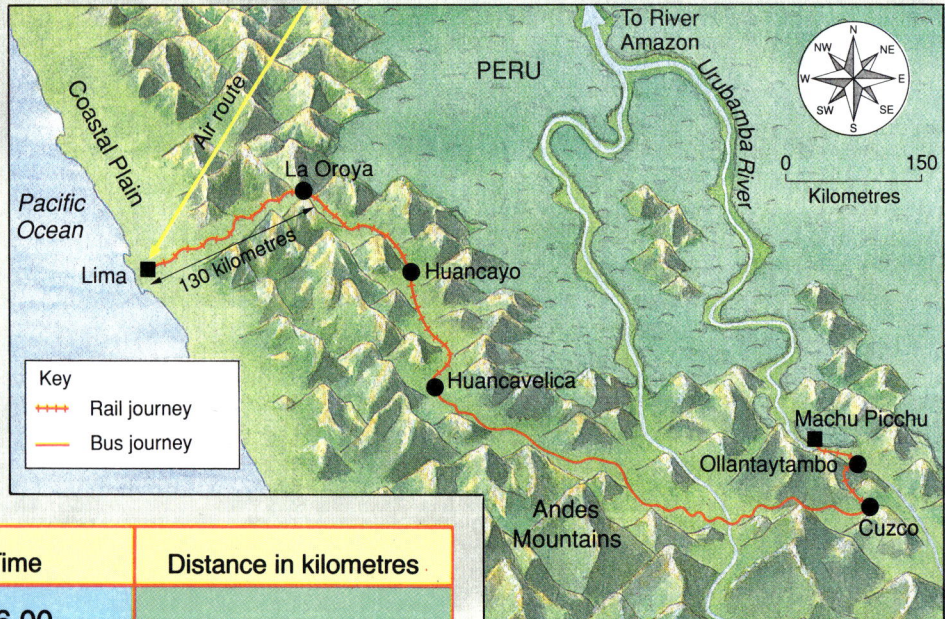

To River Amazon

PERU

Coastal Plain

Air route

Pacific Ocean

Lima

130 kilometres

La Oroya

Huancayo

Huancavelica

Urubamba River

Machu Picchu

Ollantaytambo

Cuzco

Andes Mountains

N
NW NE
W E
SW SE
S

0   150
Kilometres

Key
- ++++ Rail journey
- —— Bus journey

Place	Time	Distance in kilometres
CUZCO depart	06.00	
OLLANTAYTAMBO arrive	08.00	70
MACHU PICCHU arrive	09.40	110

At Ollantaytambo, local people are waiting at the station to sell their goods to the visitors on the train (D). They sell food, drink, clothes and other things that they make themselves.

Most of the clothes the people sell are made from llama wool. Local people keep llamas (E) for their milk and meat, as well as for wool.

D

E

Meg and Jim buy some knitted llama wool gloves at Ollantaytambo. They are feeling cold up in the high Andes mountains.

F

Soon after the train leaves Ollantaytambo, it enters the steep-sided Urubamba valley (F).

Look at C.

1a What time does the train to Ollantaytambo leave Cuzco?

1b How far is the journey from Cuzco to Machu Picchu? Is it further than the journey from Lima to La Oroya?

2 Write about what is happening in D.

G

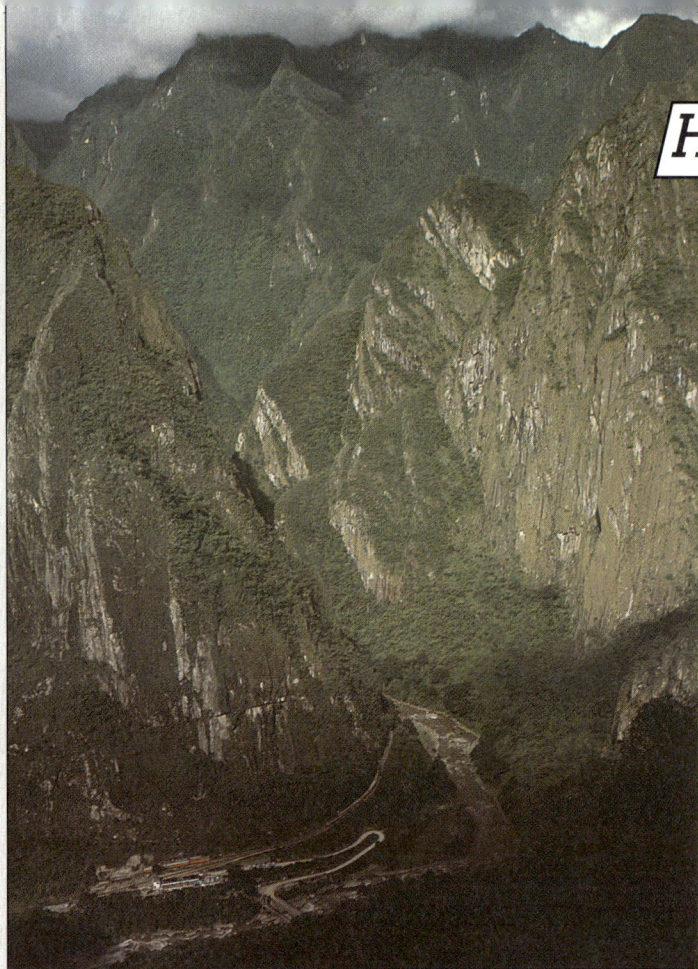

H

G was taken from high above the Urubamba valley. You can see the train on its way to Machu Picchu.

When the train arrives at Machu Picchu station (*H*), the passengers have a choice. They can walk up to the ruined city, or take a minibus up a winding road (*I*).

I

The walk takes two hours, so Meg and Jim decide to go on the bus (*J*).

J

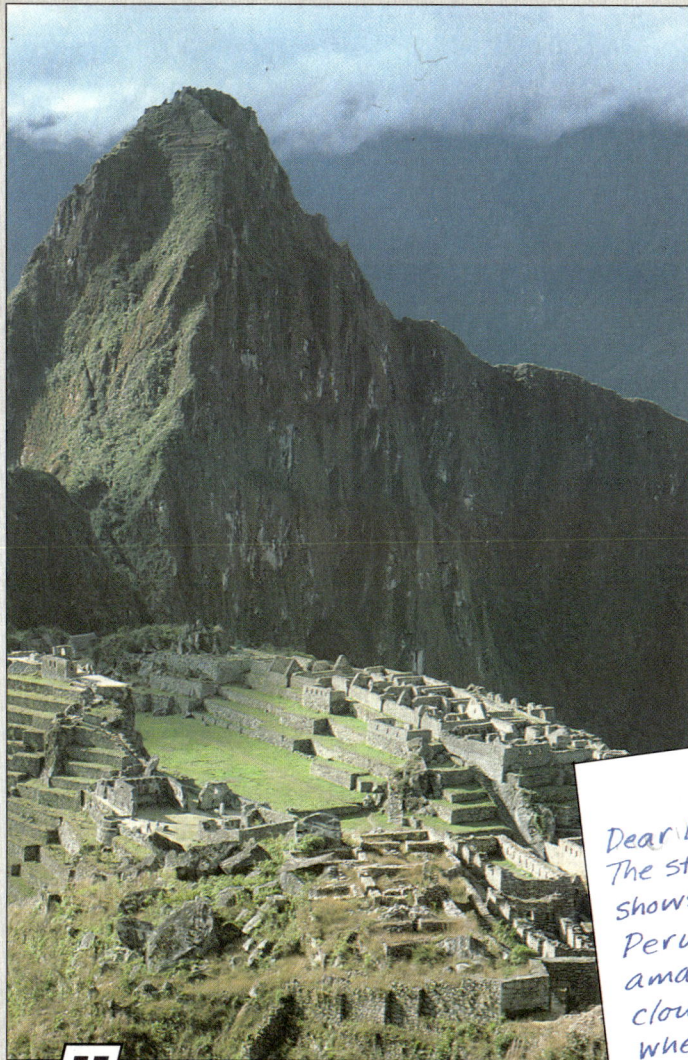

K

At last, Meg and Jim arrive at the ruined city of Machu Picchu (K). The city was built by the Incas on top of a mountain.

After the Incas left, the buildings fell down and trees grew over them. The ancient city was not discovered until 1911. Now visitors come from all over the world to see the ruins.

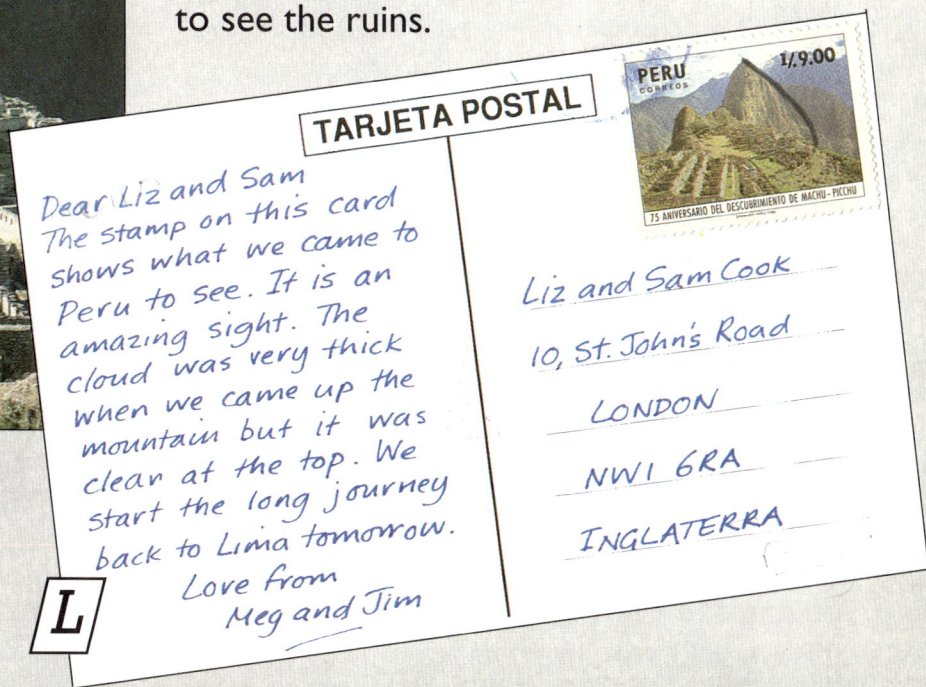

TARJETA POSTAL

PERU CORREOS I/.9.00
75 ANIVERSARIO DEL DESCUBRIMIENTO DE MACHU-PICCHU

Dear Liz and Sam
The stamp on this card shows what we came to Peru to see. It is an amazing sight. The cloud was very thick when we came up the mountain but it was clear at the top. We start the long journey back to Lima tomorrow.
Love from
Meg and Jim

Liz and Sam Cook
10, St. John's Road
LONDON
NW1 6RA
INGLATERRA

L

Look at G.

3 What did the passengers see below them out of the left side of the train?

Look at I and K.

4a Why is there no railway up the mountain to the ruined city?

4b Which way would you choose to get from Machu Picchu station to the ruined city? Why?

4c Imagine you are visiting Machu Picchu. Write a postcard to a friend.

Look at pages 62 – 68.

5 Make a list of all the towns on the journey from Lima to Machu Picchu.

6 Would you like to visit Machu Picchu? Say which parts of the journey you would like best, and which parts you would not like.

Who crosses the Channel?

The children in *A* are playing outside their school in Brussels. The main offices of the European Community are in Brussels (*B*).
Some of the people who work there send their children to the school in *A*. They come from many different countries.

Find Brussels on map *C*. This map shows the sea that separates Britain from the mainland of Europe. It is called the English Channel.

D is a photograph of the English Channel taken from France. In the background you can see the white chalk cliffs near Dover, in England.

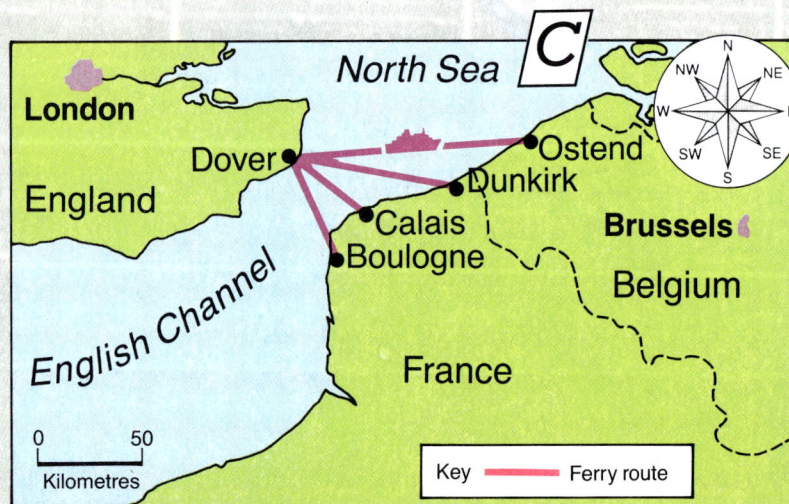

North Sea

London

Dover

England

Ostend

Dunkirk

Calais

Boulogne

English Channel

Brussels

Belgium

France

N
NW NE
W E
SW SE
S

0 50
Kilometres

Key ——— Ferry route

The Channel is a very busy crossing place. Hovercraft (*E*), ferries and aeroplanes cross it every day. They carry people, goods and vehicles.

Many people who cross the Channel are holidaymakers. Day trippers also cross to shop in the coastal towns of France or Belgium (*F*).

Day trippers who cross the Channel usually travel by ferry or by hovercraft (*E*). Other holidaymakers and business people may fly across the Channel (*G*).

Look at *C.*

1a Which ports do the Dover ferries sail to on mainland Europe?

1b List the ports in France and Belgium under two headings.
Use an atlas to list two or more channel ferry ports in England.

Look at *E*, *F* and *G.*

2a Why do people take day trips across the Channel?

2b Have you ever crossed the Channel? Write about where you were going and why.

Travelling across the Channel

The narrowest part of the Channel is called the Strait of Dover (*A*). A strait is a narrow strip of sea between two pieces of land.

On *A* you can see a tunnel marked across the strait. This is called the Channel Tunnel, or Eurotunnel. You can also see air and sea routes across the Channel.

Eurotunnel is a railway tunnel. Trains will carry vehicles and passengers through the tunnel every day (*B*).

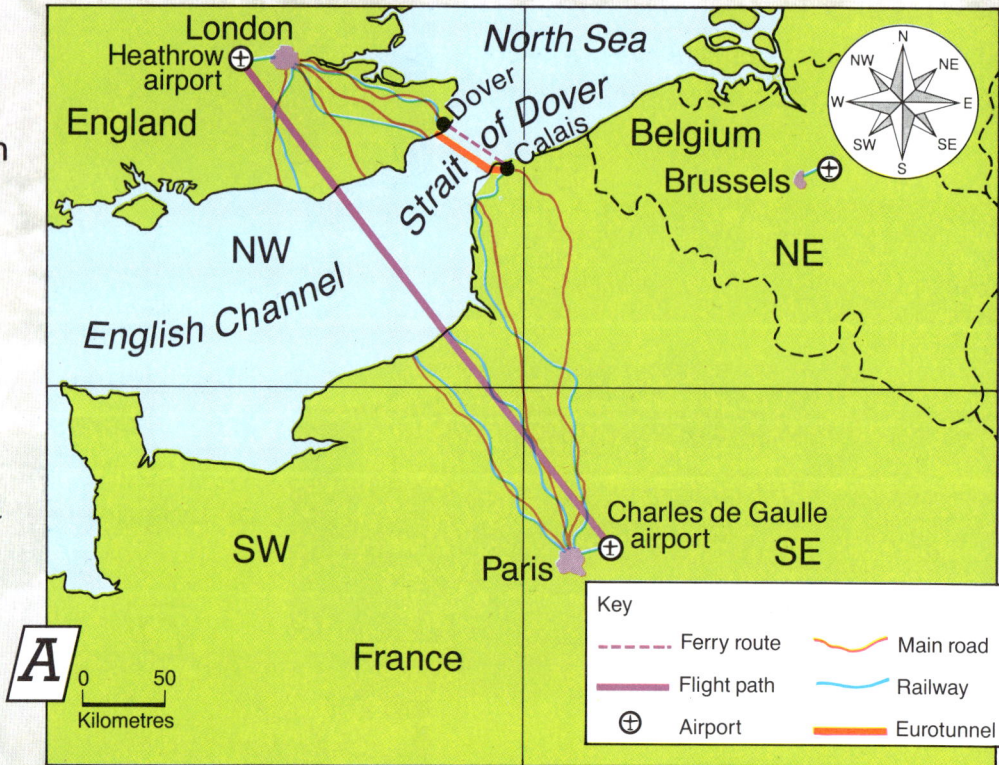

A

0   50
Kilometres

Key

----- Ferry route   Main road

----- Flight path   Railway

⊕ Airport   Eurotunnel

Vehicles driving on to tunnel trains

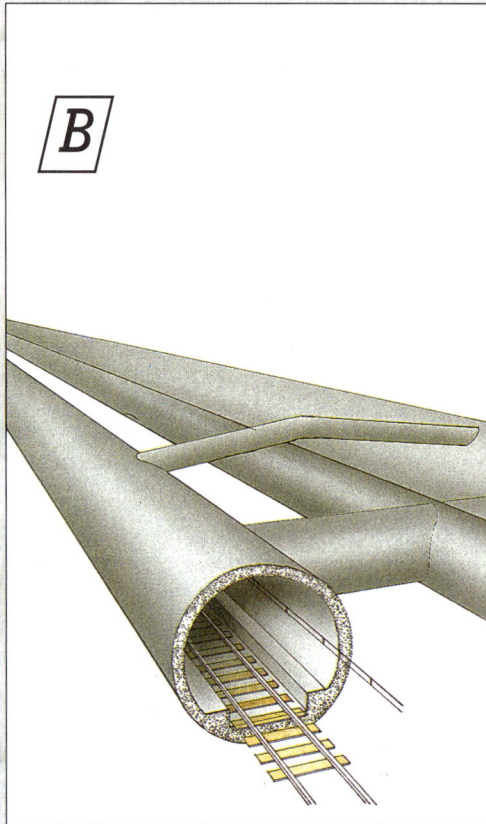

B

The Eurotunnel

In the future, a passenger will be able to travel non-stop from central London to central Paris in three hours. *C* shows how long it takes today to travel by plane and by ferry between the two city centres.

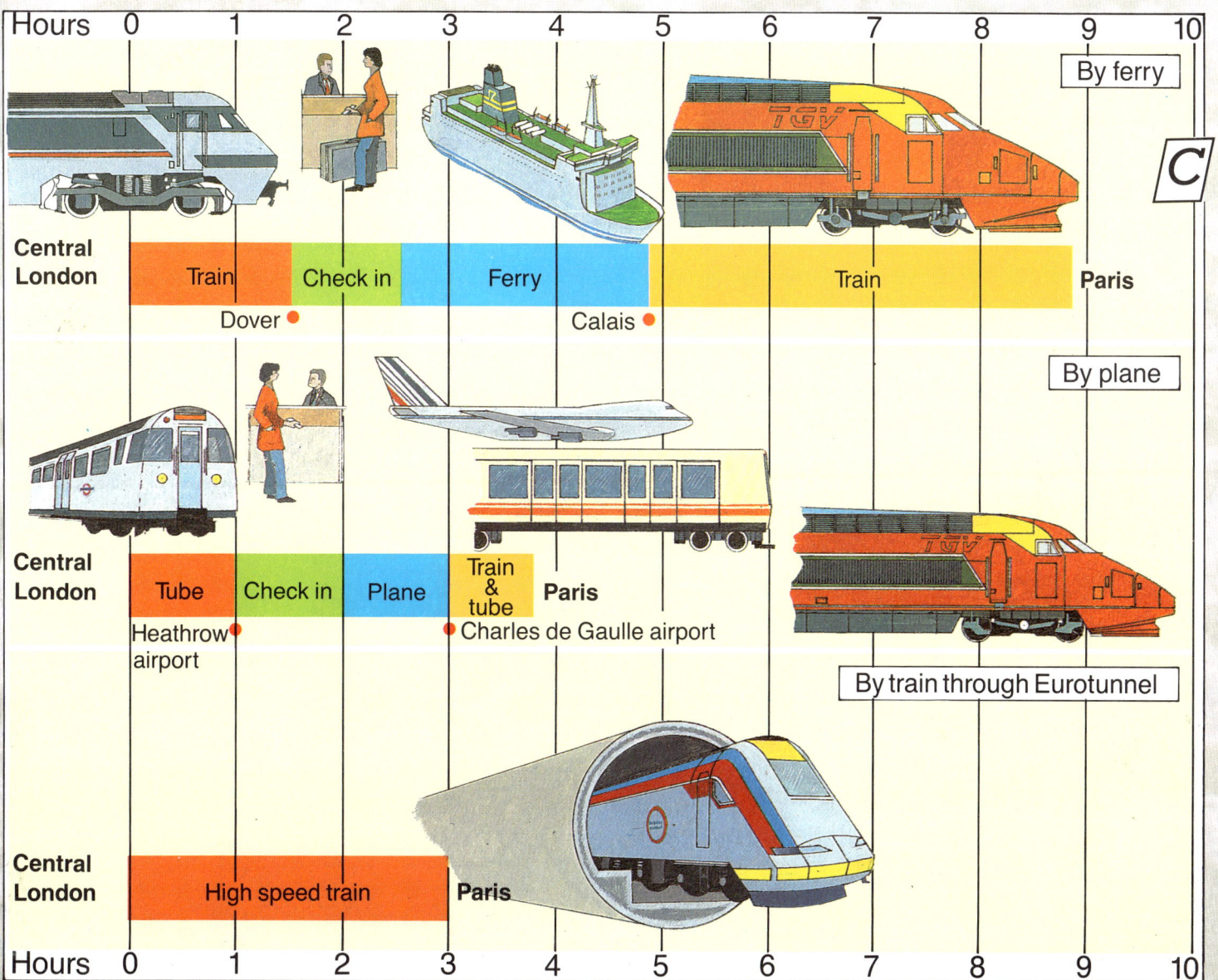

C

By ferry

| Central London | Train | Check in | Ferry | Train | Paris |

Dover ●   Calais ●

By plane

| Central London | Tube | Check in | Plane | Train & tube | Paris |

Heathrow airport ●   ● Charles de Gaulle airport

By train through Eurotunnel

| Central London | High speed train | Paris |

Look at *C*.

1a How long does it take to travel by tube train from central London to Heathrow airport?

1b How long does it take to travel from central London to Paris by air?

1c Why does the ferry journey take the most time?

1d How would you choose to travel to Paris from London? Why?

Making and using Eurotunnel

A

To make the tunnel, the builders dug under the ground from Britain and from France. In December 1990, they met in the middle (A). It was a day for the French and the British to celebrate! (B)

B

C shows one of the tunnels. It has been cut through the rock below the Strait of Dover. The rock is called chalk marl. You can see a pile of it in A.

C

D

In D you can see one of the tunnels after the walls were lined with metal. The train carries the builders to and from their work.

Chalk marl is easy to cut. It is quite soft, and water cannot pass through it.

E

Chalk cliffs of Dover

Sea bed

Chalk rock

Chalk marl rock

Cross passage

Rail tunnel

Roadway

Service tunnel

Walkway

Rail tunnel

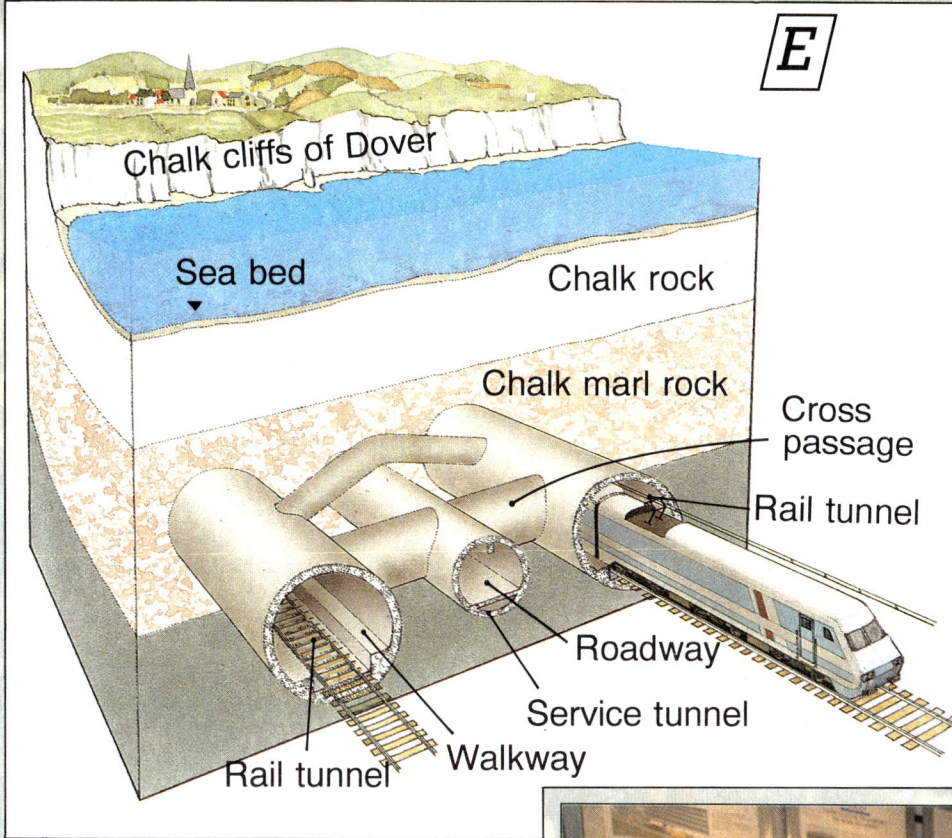

Eurotunnel is made up of three linked tunnels (*E*).

The trains travel east in one tunnel, and west in another.

The tunnel in the middle is called a service tunnel. It is linked to the rail tunnels on either side.

If a train breaks down, people can easily reach it from the service tunnel.

The boy in *F* is looking at a model of one of the Eurotunnel trains. The model is on show at the Eurotunnel Centre at Folkestone. Lots of visitors go to the Centre to find out about Eurotunnel.

F

EUROTUNNEL

Look at *E*.

1a What kind of rock are the Dover cliffs made of?

1b Why is chalk marl a good rock to make a tunnel through?

1c To which country is the train in *E* travelling?

1d In which direction will the train travel in the tunnel on the left in *E*?

1e How will the tunnel in the middle be used? What sort of tunnel is it?

Look at *F*.

2a Are the tunnel trains bigger than ordinary railway trains? Why?

2b Would you like to visit the Eurotunnel Centre? What would you like to see there?

Folkestone and Eurotunnel

A | Folkestone | M20

The entrance to the Eurotunnel in England is near the town of Folkestone. The new Eurotunnel has brought many changes to the Folkestone area.

The changes began when work on the tunnel started. Large areas of countryside were dug up and new buildings and roads were built. You can see some of these things in *A* and *B*.

Some of the people who live in Folkestone worked for ferry companies such as Sealink. Look for the Sealink ferry in *C*.

C

B

To Folkestone

Chalk cliffs

English Channel

To Dover

When Eurotunnel opens, fewer people will want to travel by ferry. In 1991, Sealink decided to close its ferry port at Folkestone. **D** shows a report of this in a local newspaper.

When the tunnel opens, there will be fewer visitors to the town. Places may close down and people will lose their jobs (*E*).

D

SEALINK CUTS JOBS AND CLOSES PORT

Sealink, Britain's second largest ferry operator, plans to cut 1500 jobs and to close the port of Folkestone in Kent. It will also cut its cross-channel route to Boulogne. This will be the end of an era. Folkestone has had a ferry service since 1842. A local resident said "It is the Channel Tunnel that has caused all this. Now Folkestone will be like a ghost town. Local shops, pubs and cafes depended on ferry passengers and workers for their trade. No-one knows what they will do now."

Some people who will lose their jobs

Ferry booking office

Local cafes and shops

Local pubs and bars

E

| Look at *A* and *B*. |

1   In what ways has Eurotunnel changed the countryside around Folkestone?

| Look at *D* and *E*. |

2a   Imagine that you live in Folkestone. Write a letter to a friend to say how you feel about the changes to your town.

2b   Look at *E* and make a list of some of the jobs that will be lost because of Eurotunnel.

2c   Why is the cat in *F* hungry?

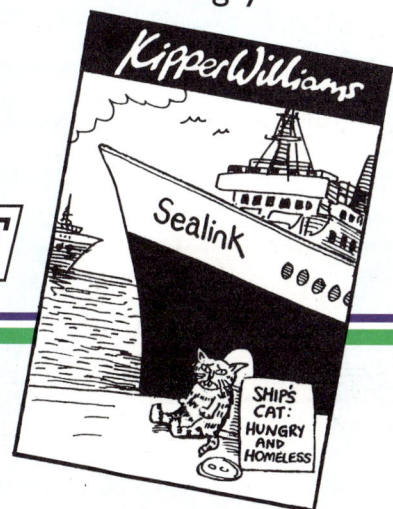

F

The European Community

A

Map key — Countries of the European Community

Labels on map:
- United Kingdom
- Ireland
- Denmark
- Netherlands
- Belgium
- Luxembourg
- Germany
- Formerly East Germany (now part of Germany)
- France
- Portugal
- Spain
- Italy
- Greece

Compass rose: N, NE, E, SE, S, SW, W, NW

Scale: 0 200 400 600 800 1000 Kilometres

Key   Countries of the European Community

■ Joined in 1953	■ Joined in 1973
	■ Joined after 1980

Eurotunnel will make it easier for people and goods to move between Britain and mainland Europe.

In 1992 twelve countries belonged to the European Community (EC). You can see these countries on map A.

The EC has its own parliament which makes rules and laws about things such as farming, fishing and industry. It also gives help to poorer parts of the community.

Fact file on Europe

Belgium

Area (in square kilometres): 33,000
Population: 9,845,000
Capital: Brussels   Population: 970,000
97 out of 100 people live in towns
Sixth richest country in the EC

Denmark

Area (in square kilometres): 43,000
Population: 5,140,000
Capital: Copenhagen   Population: 1,340,000
86 out of 100 people live in towns
Third richest country in the EC

France

Area (in square kilometres): 547,000
Population: 56,140,000
Capital: Paris   Population: 8,510,000
74 out of 100 people live in towns
Fourth richest country in the EC

Germany

Area (in square kilometres): 357,000
Population: 77,570,000
Capital: Berlin   Population: 3,000,000
82 out of 100 people live in towns
Richest country in the EC

Greece

Area (in square kilometres): 132,000
Population: 10,050,000
Capital: Athens   Population: 3,030,000
63 out of 100 people live in towns
Eleventh richest country in the EC

Ireland

Area (in square kilometres): 70,000
Population: 3,720,000
Capital: Dublin   Population: 920,000
59 out of 100 people live in towns
Tenth richest country in the EC

Italy

Area (in square kilometres): 301,000
Population: 57,100,000
Capital: Rome   Population: 2,820,000
69 out of 100 people live in towns
Seventh richest country in the EC

Luxembourg

Area (in square kilometres): 2,600
Population: 370,000
Capital: Luxembourg   Population: 77,000
83 out of 100 people live in towns
Second richest country in the EC

Netherlands

Area (in square kilometres):	37,000
Population:	14,950,000
Capital: Amsterdam Population:	1,000,000

89 out of 100 people live in towns
Fifth richest country in the EC

Portugal

Area (in square kilometres):	92,000
Population:	10,300,000
Capital: Lisbon Population:	1,610,000

33 out of 100 people live in towns
Twelfth richest country in the EC

Spain

Area (in square kilometres):	505,000
Population:	39,200,000
Capital: Madrid Population:	3,100,000

78 out of 100 people live in towns
Ninth richest country in EC

United Kingdom

Area (in square kilometres):	245,000
Population:	57,250,000
Capital: London Population:	6,770,000

93 out of 100 people live in towns
Eighth richest country in EC

Look at A on page 78.

1   Use an atlas to help you to name the countries in Europe that are not members of the EC.

Look at the Fact file.

2   Name these countries in the EC:
a) the largest in area,
b) the largest in population,
c) the country with the largest capital city,
d) the country with the largest number of people living in towns,
e) the poorest ,
f) the richest.

3   Look at the stamps of the 12 countries. Three of them show pictures of different types of farming.
a) Name the three countries these stamps come from.
b) Choose one of the three farming stamps and write about what it shows.

4   Two of the stamps show maps of the countries they come from. Name the two countries.

5   Look at the German stamp. What does the picture on it show?

6   Draw a picture for a stamp of your own country.